CW01011457

Cavalier Stronghold

Cavalier Stronghold

Ludlow in the English Civil Wars, 1642-1660

by

John Barratt

Logaston Press

LOGASTON PRESS
Little Logaston Woonton Almeley
Herefordshire HR3 6QH
logastonpress.co.uk

First published by Logaston Press 2013
Copyright © John Barratt 2013

All rights reserved. No part of this publication
may be reproduced, stored in a retrieval system,
or transmitted, in any form or by any means,
electronic, mechanical, photocopying, recording
or otherwise, without the prior permission,
in writing, of the publisher

ISBN 978 1 906663 77 3

Typeset by Logaston Press
and printed and bound in Malta
by Gutenberg Press

Contents

Acknowledgements

Thanks are due to a large number of organisations and individuals who helped in the shaping of this book.

The always helpful staff of Shropshire Archives, Shropshire Libraries, the British Library and the Bodleian Library Oxford provided help in tracing relevant items in their collections. Peter Reavill, Finds Officer at the Ludlow Museum Resources Centre, willingly shared information, theories and images on the recent dramatic discovery of the 'Bitterley Hoard'.

Also deserving of my thanks and appreciation are my always enthusiastic and supportive friends and fellow members of the Ludlow Historical Research Group. A special debt is owed to the late Dr David Lloyd, a founder member of the Group and doyen of Ludlow historians. His extensive notes on Ludlow in the Civil War, now lodged in the archives of the Historical Research Group, proved invaluable to me. Wendy Brogden kindly read the manuscript of this book, and provided many valuable insights.

Last but not least, I am indebted to Ric Tyler for his skilful interpretation of the illegible scribblings which formed the basis of the maps for this book, and to Andy Johnson of Logaston for his efficiency and forbearance!

John Barratt
Ludlow
August 2013

Preface

The Civil Wars which ravaged the British Isles in the mid-17th century are best known for their great battles, such as Edgehill, Marston Moor, Naseby and Worcester, and for the towering historical figures, Charles I, Cromwell, and so many others, who were their principal actors.

Yet the wars arguably had their greatest impact on local communities and on the daily lives of 'ordinary' people. Few towns and villages did not witness a nearby siege, battle or skirmish, or endure the demands of nearby garrisons of one or both sides. Many of their young men went, willingly or otherwise, to the wars, and often never returned, victims of a conflict whose cost in human life was proportionately as high as that of the First World War.

Ludlow was one such community. This book attempts to tell the story of this Shropshire town during those tumultuous years.

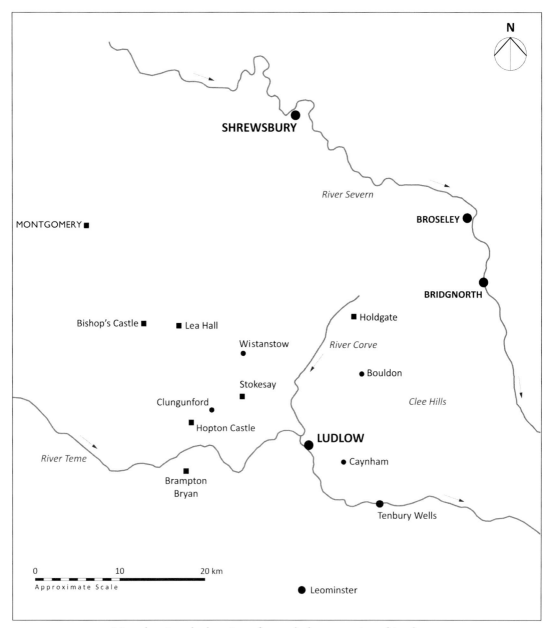

N

SHREWSBURY

River Severn

MONTGOMERY ■

BROSELEY ●

BRIDGNORTH ●

Bishop's Castle ■   ■ Lea Hall   ■ Holdgate

Wistanstow ●   *River Corve*

Stokesay ■   ● Bouldon

Clungunford ●   *Clee Hills*

■ Hopton Castle

River Teme   LUDLOW ●   ● Caynham

■   Tenbury Wells ●
Brampton
Bryan

0   10   20 km
Approximate Scale

● Leominster

Map showing the location of several places mentioned in the text

Chronology

1641

19 November	Panic over alleged Catholic attack

1642

January	King Charles leaves London
22 August	King raises standard at Nottingham in official start of war
September-October	King at Shrewsbury; Ludlow ordered to send men for army; 'battle' of Standard Oak
23 October	Battle of Edgehill
December	Ludlow Bailiffs ordered to send further levies to Shrewsbury

1643

March	First Royalist attack on Brampton Bryan
25 April	Parliamentarians under Sir William Waller occupy Hereford
May	Thomas Fisher 'governor' of Ludlow; council orders strengthening of defences
20 May	Waller evacuates Hereford
July-September	Siege of Brampton Bryan
28 September	First Battle of Newbury
October	Richard Herbert made Governor of Ludlow

1644

January	Prince Rupert appointed Lord President of the Council in the Marches and Captain General
13 March	Hopton Castle massacre
April	Siege of Brampton Bryan; Sir Michael Woodhouse appointed Governor of Ludlow
June	King Charles and Sir William Waller campaign in the West Midlands; requisitions of men and supplies made in Ludlow. Defences again strengthened
2 July	Royalist defeat at Marston Moor
18 September	Royalist defeat at Montgomery

| October-December | Unrest in south-west Shropshire in protest at activities of Van Gerris; Clubman uprising |
| 6 November | Prince Maurice made Major-General of Worcester, Shropshire, Herefordshire and Monmouth |

1645

February	Parliamentarians take Shrewsbury
March-April	Prince Rupert suppresses Clubmen
8 June	Royalists defeated near Stokesay; Stokesay Castle garrisoned by Parliamentarians
14 June	King defeated at Naseby
30 July-7 August	Scots lay siege to Hereford
23 September	Royalist defeat at Rowton Heath
1 November	Royalist defeat at Denbigh Green
18 December	Parliamentarians under John Birch capture Hereford

1646

3 February	Surrender of Chester
21 March	Royalist defeat at Stow on the Wold
24 April	Birch lays siege to Ludlow
*c.*31 May	Surrender of Ludlow
4 June	Samuel More appointed as Parliamentarian Governor of Ludlow

1 Ludlow: Town and People

'Ludlow, in Welsh Dinam and Lystwysog, that is, the Prince's Palace, is seated on a hill, at the joining of the Teme with the River Corve, a town of greater elegance than antiquity. Roger Montgomery first built here a beautiful and strong castle, hanging over the River Corve, and then enclosed it with walls about a mile in compass.'[1] Though clearly favourably impressed by what he saw, Camden was incorrect in much of what he said regarding Ludlow's origins.

There may well have been a pre-Norman settlement on or near the ridge later occupied by the town of Ludlow, but the town of the Civil War is generally accepted to have its genesis in the grant of the manor of Stanton by William fitzOsbern, companion-in-arms of William the Conqueror at Hastings, to one of his followers, Walter de Lacy.

It was de Lacy, in about 1087, who began the building of Ludlow Castle, strategically positioned on high ground overlooking the River Teme, and dominating the ford which crossed the river at Dinham. It was also Walter, or his immediate successors as lords of Ludlow, who founded the town itself. Over the next century a settlement grew up, running initially from east to west, following the line of the ridge, and then with further streets added: Broad Street and Mill Street, running downhill south to the Teme, and joined by back lanes to the older Corve and Old Streets, along which ran the road, dating back to pre-Roman times, linking Chester and Bristol by way of Shrewsbury and Hereford.[2]

Around 1199 a small Saxon church was replaced by a new building, St Laurence's, which by the 17th century had expanded into an imposing Perpendicular edifice whose tower was a landmark for many miles around.

Although there may have been earlier town defences, the stone walls which were the principal fortifications during the Civil War seem to have had their origins in the grant of murage awarded to the 'men of Ludlow' in 1233. Roughly a mile in circumference, with seven gates and several towers, the walls were probably completed in the 1260s, when there was a serious potential threat from the Welsh, though opinion is divided on whether their primary purpose was defensive or to challenge traders entering or leaving the town in order that tolls and taxes could be collected more easily.[3] The suburbs of Corve Street, Lower Broad Street and Galdeford were outside the defences, although they received some natural protection from the Teme and the Corve.

The present market place, along High Street and in Castle Square, was certainly in existence by sometime in the 12th century, with settlers encouraged by land grants or 'burgages'. Markets and fairs attracted traders from the surrounding area, with the May Fair probably the first to established.

The 14th and 15th centuries saw Ludlow at the height of its prosperity. With the Welsh wars largely at an end, trade expanded. During the 14th century Ludlow's wealth was founded on wool, from flocks in the Shropshire uplands and brought in from Wales. Ludlow merchants travelled widely, both in England and across Europe.

In the following century the town grew increasingly affluent through the manufacture of cloth, symbolised by the rebuilding of St Laurence's Church, and the numerous town houses of prosperous merchants. Along the banks of the Teme and Corve were at least nine water-powered cloth and corn mills. Despite periodic outbreaks of plague, the population slowly increased to about 1,750 in 1377.[4]

Like most English towns, Ludlow was at times caught up in political rivalry and conflict. As the enmity between the Houses of York and Lancaster flared into open warfare, Ludlow, in Yorkist territory, was engulfed in the aftermath of the otherwise virtually bloodless 'battle' of Ludford on 13 October 1459, and was sacked by the victorious Lancastrian army. But the town quickly recovered, and when Edward, Earl of March secured the throne as Edward IV in 1461, establishing the Yorkist dynasty, Ludlow would benefit from its loyalty.

Partly to strengthen control of the always unruly Welsh Marches, and also as a means of beginning his political education, the king made Ludlow Castle the residence of his eldest son, Edward, Prince of Wales, and in 1473 the Prince's Council was established in Ludlow. At a time when the cloth trade was beginning to decline, and was only partly replaced by the leather and glove industry, the arrival of the Council provided a much needed boost to the town's economy and status.[5]

After a brief hiatus following the fall of Richard III, King Henry VII re-established both the Council and the tradition of the eldest son of the monarch spending some of his formative years as its titular head in Ludlow. In 1534, following the Act of Union between England and Wales, the re-titled Council in the Marches of Wales, now tasked with administering both Wales and the former Marches, continued to make its administrative headquarters in Ludlow, with refurbishment and additional building at the Castle.

The Lord Presidents of the Council were officially based in Ludlow, though in many cases they spent little or no time there, delegating the task to their Deputy and paid officials. Longest serving was Sir Henry Sydney, who was Lord President between 1559 and 1586. Although frequently absent in Ireland and elsewhere, Sir Henry was noted for his interest in the arts, and did much to encourage the use of music in services at St Laurence's.[6]

On a day to day basis the routine work of the Council, especially of the courts whose sessions made up a major part of its role, was carried on by officials, a mixture of English and Welsh judges, lawyers, and landowning gentry from the region. The full Council rarely met, and most business was done by a small group including a senior judge who lived in the Judges Lodgings in the Castle, built, along with a bowling green and tennis court, by Sydney in the 1580s. Other salaried officials also lived in the town, among them Charles Fox, Secretary to the Council, who built a fine house in what is now Quality Square, and Rhys Jones, a Welsh attorney whose house in Corve Street later became The Feathers.

Visiting lawyers, officials, and plaintiffs at the courts resulted in a 'great access of strangers out of all the principality of Wales and the Marches'.[7] Ludlow's inns in particular, such as The Crown and The Angel in Broad Street, prospered as a result, and many officials rented long-term lodgings in the town.

Local tradesmen benefited from supplying the needs of the Council, ranging from basics such as cloth and food, through to the more esoteric, such as 'sweet water and damaske powder to perfume the rooms of my lord's lady coming from London'.[8] Local labour was employed for repairs and building work at the castle, and townspeople supplied many of the daily needs of the Council, among them Elizabeth Butler, a widow, who in 1603 was paid £8 8s 'for washing linen'. In 1615-16, Thomas Griffiths was paid 15s for 'killing noisome vermin as rats and mice in Ludlow castle', and Michael Adams received 12s for various tasks, including repairing the coat of arms over the castle gate.[9]

The Feathers', formerly the 'Falcon Inn' before being reconstructed early in the 17th century as the residence of Rhys Jones, Attorney to the Council in the Marches. This building was typical of the Ludlow town houses of the Council's leading officials.

Although the townspeople were perhaps not directly involved in some of the entertainments of the leading members of the Council, such as the performance at the castle of John Milton's *Comus* in 1634, the interaction which did take place between town and Council was illustrated visually by the tombs of a number of Council officials in St Laurence's Church, and by their residences in Ludlow.

To some extent the officials of the Council took on the role of the 'old' nobility, who owned little land in the Ludlow area, with no paramount county magnate in Shropshire. The earl of Bridgewater, who was President of the Council until its abolition in 1642, rarely visited the town, and as was usual exercised his duties by means of deputies. As a result he had little real influence in the town, and failed in an attempt to have his son elected as one of Ludlow's two MPs.[10]

Not everyone in Ludlow found the presence of the Council entirely welcome. With its retinue of officials and petitioners, the Council took on some of the customs and vices of its royal Court in London. The Puritan divine Richard Baxter, who as a teenager lived in Ludlow, admitted that he had been urged on by his contemporaries to indulge in gambling: 'idle gentlemen had little else to do ... The town was full of temptations through the multitude of persons (counsellors, attorneys, officers and clerks) and much given to tippling and excess.'[11] In 1626 cognisances to sell beer and ale were granted to around 100 Ludlovians, although only 16 of them kept inns distinguished by a sign.[12]

Much of this 'excess' was no doubt beneficial to the town financially, and the Council certainly played an important role in shielding Ludlow from some of the worst effects of economic recession. In 1545 the population of the town was estimated at 2,500, placing Ludlow quite high up the scale of England's 7-800 medium sized and small towns, though in fact the total population had declined from around 3,300 earlier in the century. The survey of the former property in the town of the Palmers' Guild carried out in 1551 lists a significant number of untenanted or 'decayed' properties.

As well as the decline of the cloth trade, disease and the effects of poor harvests played a part in population fluctuations. Like the rest of the country, Ludlow was subject to the periodic ravages of plague. It struck in 1597, and again in 1608-9, when 104 people died. There were further outbreaks in 1623-4 and 1636. It was usually the young who suffered the highest rates of mortality, and with knowledge of hygiene and prevention at best rudimentary, little could be done to try to curb the epidemics other than by isolating those affected in their homes – termed 'plague houses'.[13]

Early in the 17th century Ludlow was predominantly a market town, relying on the surrounding countryside for much of its food, in the form of meat, fish and wheat, bought and sold at the regular fairs and weekly markets. Many of the townspeople who followed occupations such as leather working and glove making were also part-time farmers, raising cattle and sheep, sometimes as far away as mid-Wales. The town fields, medieval in origin, such as those at Hucklemarsh and Waretree Field near Gallows Bank, were still used by the inhabitants for crop growing, mainly corn and oats, and they also kept cattle, sheep and pigs. Largely because of the survival of the original burgage plots, often up to 300 feet in length, which had been granted to the medieval settlers of Ludlow, many houses within the town had long gardens at their rear in which there were orchards and vegetable plots, and where pigs and poultry were kept.

The principal town market was held on Monday, attracting traders from a wide area of the West Midlands, and also street entertainers of various kinds. Fairs were held each year, on the former feast days of St Laurence (August 10), St Catherine (November 25), Whitsun and St Lambert (September 17). The corporation administered the fairs and markets, taking rents for the stalls, levying various tolls and fining those who transgressed the market regulations.

Traders from elsewhere were not always welcomed, especially if they attempted to sell goods already available from Ludlow stall holders. Others came from a considerable distance, as did many of the buyers, from the West Midlands and Wales, especially for livestock, which were sold from enclosures at the Bull Ring, Corve Street and Old Street end of the market.

Most of the items on sale, such as salt and thread, were provided by traders from Ludlow itself, or from the surrounding villages. Although most of these goods were sold in the market place on High Street, there was also a small market hall in Castle Square, built around 1556-7. Corn and oats were sold here, with some other items such as hardware.[14]

Around a third of the male population of Ludlow worked in the cloth trade and, at its peak, about a quarter were engaged in the leather trade, especially as cobblers, glovers and saddlers. Their activities were carefully regulated by various trade guilds, often by this time amalgamations of associated crafts. The Guild of Hammermen included around 26 trades, among them carpenters, joiners, smiths, glaziers and cutlers. The Stitchmen numbered in their ranks drapers, tailors, mercers and hatters. There were also distinct guilds, among them those of the butchers and cobblers.

The guilds strictly regulated their particular trades in the interests of their members, and would take legal action against traders not admitted to their ranks. They would also provide some financial assistance to members in difficulties. The guilds, whose meetings were often held in St Laurence's Church, were run by small groups of elected officials, some of whom were also members of the corporation.

The principal trades, especially the clothiers, employed large numbers of homeworkers, such as spinners and carders. At the beginning of the 17th century, many of the leading clothier families such as the Hooks and Blashfields were locally very influential, mostly living and running their businesses in the centre of the town, often with imposing premises. Many of them exerted further influence through membership of the town council. However, the clothing industry went into steady decline after 1600 because of cheaper competition from East Anglia, better-placed for trade with London and the south-east, and from the 'new drapieries' originating in Europe. Some of the fulling mills on the banks of the rivers were converted to milling corn.[15]

Ludlow lay astride the main routes from Wales to the south midlands and Worcester and eventually London, and on the main north-south route between Bristol and Chester. Given the frequently appalling state of even major roads, river transport was of paramount importance to the 17th-century economy. The River Severn to the east of Ludlow was a major artery, and was used to transport goods from Bristol as far upstream as Bewdley, from where they had to be moved overland. Although in 1636 the Privy Council in London supported a proposal to make part of the River Teme navigable, this came to nothing, and Ludlow remained dependent on land communications. As a result it was an important centre of the carrying trade, with wagons and carriers transporting goods across a wide area. In 1682 the business operated by Francis Ball and Edward Miles of Mill Street had 18 wagons and teams of horses. There was also a regular and rapid letter carrying service to and from London, often taking no more than two days.[16]

Housing in Ludlow reflected the sharp divisions in wealth and status. The homes of the more prosperous merchants and traders, and officials of the Council in the Marches, gave visible evidence of their position. In many cases they were medieval houses, extensively rebuilt, with three or four floors, especially after 1600, in half-timbered style with overhanging upper floors to demonstrate the status of their owners, as for example in Tamburlaine House. Thomas Churchyard on visiting the town wrote in 1587: 'On every side thereof fair houses are. That makes a show to please both mind and eye.' In some cases buildings, as with the original medieval open shops and stalls, had first been enclosed, and then had an upper storey added as living quarters.[17]

There were, however, particularly in the suburbs of Galdeford and Lower Broad Street, the often fairly wretched dwellings of those living in acute poverty. It was not unknown for the poor and homeless to die from extreme cold in the street. The corporation provided some help to those in need, albeit in a rather haphazard way, and often concentrated upon those related to or known by them.[18]

In the hundred years after 1541 the economic pull of the Council in the Marches was largely offset by the town's relatively high mortality rate and on the eve of the Civil War, in 1641, the population totalled around 2,600, just a hundred more than a century previously. Of these around 700 were adult males, with between 500 and 600 of them of military age.[19]

Ludlow was administered by the borough corporation which consisted of 12 aldermen and 25 common councillors, sometimes termed 'the Twelve and Twenty-five'. As with most town councils of the time, the Ludlow corporation was an oligarchy, self-electing new members to fill vacancies by means of a process that offered limited input from the burgesses of the town. Councillors generally remained in office for life. The aldermen were chosen from the 25 common councillors, the common councillors from among the 'burgesses' – usually the higher echelons of local society – the councillors often being members of the cloth and leather trades or other leading merchants, and often relatives of existing councillors.

The civic year commenced on the festival of St Simon and St Jude, when the council's principal elected officers, the High and Low Bailiffs, the Chamberlain and High Constable, were chosen with both the latter posts often held by the same individual. The High Bailiff was selected from among the aldermen, the Low Bailiff from the common councillors. The bailiffs were the principal administrative officers of the council, with considerable decision-making power and responsibility, including the power to try criminal cases, and until 1627, the authority to pass sentences of death or mutilation.

The Town Court had been established by the Charter of 1461, and tried a wide variety of cases, though after 1626 capital sentences could only be passed if the Recorder was present, and there was a gibbet standing as a permanent visible deterrent on Gallows Bank overlooking the town. More common were charges such as drunkenness and brawling. A whipping post was in place near the Market House, and on occasion miscreants were flogged through the town tied behind a cart. There were movable stocks, and no town of the period was complete without its ducking stool, to which, for example, Mary Derby of Lower Broad Street was sentenced in 1600 as 'a drunkard, swearer, curser and common scold'.[20]

As the aldermen were normally selected from those of the common councillors who had previously been Low Bailiffs, the result was an oligarchy within an oligarchy. Unsurprisingly, there were periodic accusations from those outside the ruling circles of corruption and nepotism, especially when some individuals or members of the same family held office successively or repeatedly, though there is little to suggest that Ludlow was worse in this respect than other places. Occasionally such disputes emerged among the ranks of the council itself. In 1630 councillor Thomas Edwards was sequestered from the council after accusing Bailiff Thomas Collerick of being 'led home drunk Monday last'.[21]

Another important role in civic life was that of the Chamberlain, who was responsible for accounting for corporation rents and expenditure. The main sources of income of the corporation came from the demesne lands and property in the town, which by 1619 brought in rents totalling over £200 a year. Added to this was income from tolls, fines, and the 12d payable annually by the holder of each burgage plot in the town, with the result that Ludlow corporation was relatively wealthy.

A High Constable was responsible for the town gaol, which was located in the tower of Galdeford Gate. Subordinate to him were town constables, elected from each ward of the town, who dealt with day to day policing matters. Two sergeants of mace and a common sergeant, salaried officials, dealt with the upkeep of the gaol and also assisted in maintaining discipline in the town. Also salaried was the Town Clerk. Not directly appointed by the council were the churchwardens – often young men regarded as potential future common councillors, and serving a kind of apprenticeship.

The council was also responsible for a variety of other functions. Administration of the poor law, the upkeep of street paving, public wells and conduits, organization of some building repairs and provision of a basic public health system fell within its remit, although it concentrated most of its time on its property ownership and financial matters.[22]

Though certainly guilty of corruption and malpractice at times, the corporation was also capable of presenting an imposing public ceremony. One such, perhaps remembered with distinctly mixed feelings in later years, was the event to mark the proclamation of Charles, King James I's eldest son, as Prince of Wales on 4 November 1616.

The ceremony was splendidly attended by Sir Thomas Chamberlain, Chief Justice of Chester, the High Sheriff and 'many thousand' of the gentry of Shropshire, the Marches and north Wales. At nine o'clock in the morning, the Town Bailiffs, William Gregory and Thomas Blashfield, with the mace bearers and the remainder of the corporation 'very richly clad and apparelled', the church choir singing psalms and hymns, and young men from the Free School, carrying 'several pennons and Bannerolls of the Arms and Achievements of our said Prince Charles' made their way in procession to the castle. Ahead of them the 'Town Waites and other loud Instruments of Musick marched along the number of two hundred soldiers with Halberds, Pikes, Corslets, Muskets and Calivers ...'. The latter were presumably men of the Ludlow and neighbouring Trained Band (see chapter 3).

At the castle the town dignitaries met up with the officials of the Council in the Marches, and 'a great Volley of shot was fired which so pierced the Air with the great noise of Drums and sound of Trumpets, Fifes, Flutes and other instruments, as the like in these parts hath not been seen ... and marshalling themselves in good array they all went through the Town Streets to the church ...'

A service followed, with a sermon lasting an hour and a half, following which the dignitaries repaired to the market place, near the High Cross (on the site of the present Buttercross). Here, on a specially erected platform:

> ... the said scholars with their Penons ... in their hands ascended; and as the said Justice and Counsell passed by ... uttered and pronounced ... several Speeches ... All of which were principally invented and made by the painful industry of Humfrey Herbert Chief Schoolmaster of His Majesty's Free School there ...
>
> And then, being full one of the clock in the afternoon, the said Justice and Council, with the Knights, Esquires, and best sort of Gentlemen returned into the Castle to dinner where was a great Feast provided ... the Bailiffs also with their Bretheren and Burgesses went down to the Town, to spend the rest of the day in all joyful and jovial manner ... having all drunk plentifully of wine by appointment of [the] chief Steward to the King's Household there ...

Though rather pointedly uninvited to the 'Feast' at the castle, the corporation was involved in further celebrations next day, 5 November:

> The Bailiffs ... humbly taking their leave ... Master Justice required them ... to express their joy ... for our said Sovereign's Deliverance from the Papist's treasonable and horrible conspiracy ... and to be in readiness with the ... Justice and Council the next morning ... to praise God for the same ... Which accordingly was performed the next day... the Music, Ringing and Bonfires continuing ... all the said day.[23]

Few would have believed that 30 years later, Ludlow, with the rest of the British Isles, would be in the grip of Civil War.

2 THE ROAD TO WAR

Many volumes have been written in an attempt to analyse the causes of the civil wars of the 17th century, but the debate continues. In broad terms, the desire of the Stuart kings, particularly King Charles I, to establish a centralised government focused on the monarchy, emphasised by their belief in the 'Divine Right of Kings' – the monarch as God's Deputy on Earth, and ultimately answerable only to Him – set them eventually on a collision course with the vested interests of magnates, gentry, merchants and professional classes represented by Parliament. In 1629 King Charles dismissed his Parliament and embarked on his period of 'personal rule', which continued, generally rather more successfully than sometimes suggested, for the next eleven years.[1]

King Charles I (1600-49). Charles had many faults, notably a mixture of stubbornness and hesitancy, both usually displayed at the wrong time. Personally brave, there is little evidence that Charles possessed any notable ability as a general.

Raising the necessary revenue without a Parliament to authorise taxation was an ongoing problem, and resulted in the king and his ministers resorting to unpopular measures such as extending the tax known as 'Ship Money', theoretically originally intended for maritime defence and levied in coastal counties, to inland areas. This and similar expedients were resented, but religion was to prove to be a greater flashpoint.

Though there were significant catholic minorities in several parts of the kingdom, and in Ireland an overwhelming majority, the bulk of the population was solidly protestant. The determination of King

Charles and Archbishop Laud to introduce a more rigidly hierarchical structure in the Church of England, together with more ceremonial and ornamentation, therefore suggested to many a plan to re-introduce catholicism through the back door.

These religious policies were generally accepted in England and Wales, albeit in rather luke-warm fashion, apart from by the Puritan minority. But the situation in Presbyterian Scotland was very different. The attempt by Charles and his Scottish bishops to impose the Anglican version of his church there, as well as proposals to recover church lands in the possession of the Scottish nobility since the Reformation, resulted in opposition groups north of the border uniting in signing the National Covenant, pledging rejection of the religious reforms.

From then onwards, the drift to a civil war which few would have envisaged had begun. In 1639 and 1640, ill-judged attempts by the king to impose his will on the Scots by force in the largely bloodless 'Bishops' Wars' ended in ignominious failure for Charles, and saw a Scottish army in occupation of much of the north of England.

Faced by a major financial crisis, as well as by the need to buy off the Scots, Charles was forced to recall Parliament. Rather than concern for the plight in which the king had placed himself, what became known as the Long Parliament, representing the protestant aristocratic and mercantile classes of England, saw their opportunity to force concessions from Charles, and to claw back the encroaching powers which he had gained during the years of personal rule.

At this stage few if any of the king's opponents aimed at his deposition, nor would most do so for many years to come. But their attitude towards his principal advisers was unforgiving. The Earl of Strafford, Charles' chief minister, was impeached and tried on dubious allegations of having proposed to bring in an army from Ireland to crush the king's English opponents. He was found guilty, and the reluctant monarch was forced to acquiesce in his execution. Strafford was soon followed to the Tower of London by Archbishop Laud.

An already inflamed situation was worsened in October 1641 by the outbreak of rebellion in Ireland. Reports of widespread massacres of protestant settlers were brought across the Irish Sea by waves of refugees. These claims were greatly exaggerated in the process, but this counted for little and wild rumours of planned catholic uprisings on the mainland swept across England and Wales. An army was needed to fight the rebellion, and, amid allegations that King Charles was in league with the Irish rebels, the majority in Parliament were determined that the troops raised should not be under his command. Demands that Parliament should have control of the militia, hitherto a royal prerogative, were added to a range of other concessions demanded.

Matters came to a head in January 1642 when King Charles and a group of armed supporters entered Parliament in an attempt to arrest the 'Five Members' – leading Parliamentarian opponents of the king. The attempt failed, and soon afterwards, faced by an increasingly hostile capital, Charles left London, heading first to Windsor and then to York, where his leading supporters began to rally to him. As summer approached, and the positions of both king and Parliament hardened, civil war became inevitable.[2]

There is little to suggest that Ludlovians initially took a very partisan position regarding the controversial issues of the years of personal rule. In general, so far as the religious changes initiated by Charles and Archbishop Laud were concerned, Ludlow conformed, albeit unenthusiastically. There was certainly a Puritan element among the town's population, and they made occasional generally low-key protests against the changes in religious ceremonial in St Laurence's, and were brought before the ecclesiastical court on charges such as not removing their hats during services. There were also Catholics in the town; the Townsend family were known recusants, as was the Secretary to the Council in the Marches, Charles Fox. However, apart from periodically being fined for non-church attendance, Ludlow's Catholics conformed sufficiently to avoid prosecution, or were tacitly tolerated.

Most of the cases brought before the ecclesiastical court involved breaches of morality or disorder in church. In what may have been a personal rather than theological disagreement, Rector James Crowther brought Edward Leigh before the court 'for railing at him with reviling words' – "Go, goosecrap fool – a fart for you".' Other offences noted were swearing in church, 'evil demeanour', playing cards or drinking during the time of church service, or being otherwise absent without reasonable excuse.[3]

To some extent the attitude of the church must have been influenced by the view of the successive rectors of Ludlow. In 1637 Richard Fletcher, an Oxford graduate who had been headmaster of the Ludlow grammar school since 1624, was appointed rector. It may be that he took a more uncompromising approach, or simply that he knew his parishioners rather well, for there do appear to have been an increasing number of cases brought before the ecclesiastical court in the years leading up to the Civil War. They were accused of the usual array of misdemeanours, including having illegitimate children. The more influential were usually able to make recompense by payment of a fine or by private penance, but others were made to appear, wearing a white sheet and carrying a wand, either before the congregation or in the marketplace.

It does not appear that either the authorities at St Laurence's or the town council displayed any particular energy in putting Laudian

St Laurence's Church Ludlow. Testimony to the wealth of Ludlow during medieval times, St Laurence's bells were rung in celebration of Royalist victories during the war, and it also witnessed the burials of many of their dead.

theological changes into practice. Those which did take place were probably more the result of the influence of the Council in the Marches reflecting government policy. They included various decorative changes, and a continued emphasis on church music, with paid organist and choir. But it is perhaps significant that St Laurence's seems to have continued to employ an unmarked communion table, not the decorated altar which Laud specified should be used.[4]

The low-key approach to religious controversy which was prevalent in Ludlow in the pre-war years was mirrored in the attitude of the majority towards political change. Shropshire in general was a conservative society, its towns generally too small, and too far from London, to be caught up in the increasingly heated disputes taking place between king and Parliament.

The chief political activist in the area was Sir Robert Harley of Brampton Bryan in Herefordshire, six miles south-west of Ludlow. A fervent and apparently humourless Puritan, Harley, aged 63 in 1642, was a leading opponent of the king in Parliament, and when war broke out two of his sons would take commissions in the Parliamentarian armies. However Harley had little influence in Ludlow, and seems to have been personally unpopular there.

Sir Robert Harley (1579-1656).
The leading Parliamentarian supporter in the Ludlow area, Sir Robert was absent in London for most the war, and would later become an opponent of the Commonwealth and Cromwell's Protectorate.

Ludlow returned two MPs to Parliament. They were rarely townsmen, more usually former officials of the Council in the Marches or neighbouring country gentry, and therefore likely to favour the conservative viewpoint. In the Long Parliament of 1640 Ludlow was represented by Ralph Goodwin and Charles Baldwin. Baldwin came from a family which had held lands at Elsich in nearby Corvedale for 200 years, and he had been a Ludlow councillor in 1639. Goodwin, described as 'a man of learning and a poet', had been in the service of the Earl of Bridgewater, Lord President of the Council in the Marches, but had quarrelled with him, despite which he had been re-elected as MP. Both would be Royalist supporters during the Civil War.[5]

But the degree of political apathy in Ludlow can be overstated. The unpopular Ship Money tax aroused significant opposition in the town. In 1637 the High Sheriff of Shropshire complained to the Privy Council in London that Ludlow had paid none of the £102 for which it had been assessed, and was 'the worst place in the county'. This reluctance seems in part to have resulted from a successful appeal by Shrewsbury to the Privy Council regarding the sum demanded from it. The Privy Council upheld the appeal, and £28 of the assessment was added to Ludlow's bill. It appears though that the demanded amount was eventually paid.[6]

Another bone of contention resulted from an ongoing dispute regarding the town mills. These, for corn grinding and cloth fulling, had been numerous in medieval times, but by the early years of the 17th century were in decline. The most important of those still in use were the two castle mills, usually rented from the corporation. A dispute arose in 1634 when Alexander Gretton, Clerk of Spices in the royal household, was granted, as a result of complex medieval property divisions (known as the 'moities') between the town and the crown, the income from five of Ludlow's corn mills. Ludlow's corporation argued its own claims in court, but lost. It incurred heavy legal costs and the corporation tenants of the mills in question were dispossessed.[7]

The outbreak of the Bishops' Wars brought further grievances. Although it is unlikely that any Ludlow men actually saw action in the armies which Charles raised for his brief and almost bloodless campaigns, the town was called on to help meet the costs incurred. The reluctance which had been apparent in the payment of Ship Money was again noticeable. In 1640 Ludlow's contribution to 'Coat and Conduct Money' was short by £40.

1641 was to see opinion coalesce sharply when, in the spring, Parliament, as part of its raft of reforms, proposed the abolition of the Council in the Marches. Whilst the townspeople of Ludlow had not always been on the best of terms with the Council, they recognised the important role which it played in the economy of the town, and the proposed abolition was met with alarm. The corporation petitioned Parliament that it would cause 'the utter ruin of a thousand poor souls'. Ludlow's MP, Charles Baldwin, promised to do 'what I can for your Corporation'. But all protests were in vain and the Council in the Marches was abolished in August 1641.[8]

Growing tensions were fanned by news of the rebellion in Ireland, and in November rumours of an imminent catholic uprising swept the region. All through the night of 19 November the townsmen of Ludlow, along with those of Kidderminster and Bridgnorth, stood to arms in expectation of an attack. Nothing happened, and it was felt by many that Sir Robert Harley, who was thought to be the source of the alarm, was actually motivated by fears of an attack on Brampton Bryan Castle. Harley had written to Ludlow council: 'Look well to your town, for the Papists are discovered to have a bloody design in general, as well against this Kingdom as elsewhere.'[9]

Although by the summer of 1642 opinion in Ludlow, as much from selfish reasons as from sentiment or political conviction, was hardening in support of King Charles, there were of course those in the town who favoured the Parliamentarian side. Not a great deal is known about them, but they seem to have been headed by John Aston who had been one of the bailiffs in 1640. He had been in the forefront of the opposition to the payment of 'Coat and Conduct Money', refusing to hand over £6 which had been raised, or to provide horses for officers of troops levied in Brecknock and Herefordshire. He was also suspected to have acted as Harley's agent in the catholic rebellion scare of 1641.[10]

But as the last hopes of peace dwindled and died that summer, the overwhelming hope of the people of Ludlow as in many other parts of the kingdom, was that the impending conflict between king and Parliament would leave them unscathed, and be ended by one decisive battle.

3   ARMS AND THE MAN

In the summer of 1642, England and Wales had witnessed no major acts of warfare for over a century. Most English towns and cities had expanded beyond any medieval walls they may have possessed, and in any case the walls were increasingly ineffective against the power of siege artillery, and as a result had usually been allowed to fall into decay. Apart from a small number of garrisons, such as Berwick on the turbulent border with Scotland, and a few naval bases like Portsmouth, there was no standing army. England's first line of defence was still, as in the days of Queen Elizabeth I, at sea.

The second line of defence was to be provided by the militia or 'posse comitatus'. In theory the entire male population between the ages of 16 and 60 was liable to be called up by the county sheriffs for military service in times of national emergency. But the Tudor regime, always fearful of rebellion, had been uneasy at the prospect of relying entirely upon such a universal force of uncertain loyalty, which might potentially present a threat to the established social and political order. Rather than depend on the militia, a new part-time force, known as the Trained Bands, was set up. Drawn from what were seen as the more responsible sections of society, they were to be 'men sufficient, of able and active bodies; none of the meaner sort or servants but only such as be of the Gentry, Free-holders and good Farmers, or their sons, that are like to be resident'. In towns such as Ludlow, they would be drawn from the merchant, official and more prosperous tradesmen classes of the population, seen as having a stake in the continued stability of the social order.

The recruits were 'to meet to be sorted into bands, and to be trained and exercised in such sort as may reasonably be borne by a common charge of the whole county'. Each shire's Lord Lieutenant and his deputies were presented with a figure for the total number of men the central government expected them to raise, and were required in turn to set a quota to be produced by each town and locality. These were normally formed into individual companies, commanded by locally influential gentry or important townsmen, sometimes with a professional soldier hired to train them.

The degree of training and efficiency of the Bands varied considerably. In areas deemed to be under potential threat, such as the south coast or the Scottish border, both drill and equipment were given higher priority than was the case in inland areas apparently far from any military threat.

The Trained Bands, like the militia, were intended for home defence, which was generally unofficially interpreted as being in their home county rather than further afield. On a few occasions, notably the Elizabethan wars with Spain and in Ireland in the 1590s, some Trained

Bandsmen had served overseas, but this was highly unusual, and generally viewed as being illegal. In practice, as both king and Parliament discovered in 1642 when trying to muster the Trained Bands in their support, much depended upon the attitude of local commanders – and even more upon that of their men. Although in 1638 the Trained Bands of England and Wales were reckoned to total 93,718 foot and 5,239 horse, their actual military capabilities were much less than these figures might suggest.[1]

Each county had a muster-master, paid for by the crown, and responsible, with deputies, for training. The results were decidedly mixed. The London Trained Bands were a rare exception, well-trained, and willing, with reservations, to serve away from the capital. They were to prove a very significant addition to the Parliamentarian armies. But they had few counterparts. In most cases enthusiasm for training and willingness to pay for arms and equipment were at best luke-warm, and training days became rather more social occasions than serious military under-takings. In 1635 the military writer, Robert Ward, commented bitterly that training sessions were 'matters of disport and things of no moment'. Such evidence as survives suggests that the Shropshire Trained Bands would not have met with Ward's approbation.[2]

This apparent lack of military preparedness has led many writers to see the English Civil War as a clash between amateur armies. However, this was only partly the case. There was actu-ally a substantial reservoir of military experience to be tapped into.

The long-standing religious conflicts in Europe did not affect the British Isles directly until the Bishops' Wars of 1639 and 1640, and the outbreak of rebellion in Ireland in the following year. But thousands of men from the 'Three Kingdoms' of the British Isles saw service in Europe. A short period of military experience, most commonly in the armies of the protestant Dutch Low Countries, but occasionally, in the case of Catholics, with their Spanish and Impe-rialist opponents, was seen as a desirable part of the education of the English gentry classes. Some, usually younger sons or individuals who for various reasons felt it wise to be out of the country for a while, became professional soldiers, either permanently or for a number of years. English and, especially, Scots regiments were raised to serve with the Dutch forces, and there was even an English unit with the Spanish Army of Flanders. Still others, albeit reluctantly, saw brief military service in King Charles' ill-fated Bishops' Wars, whilst the outbreak of rebellion in Ireland, and the raising of troops in England and Wales to combat it, attracted many profes-sional soldiers back from the Continent.

Thus, on the outbreak of civil war in England and Wales, there were considerable numbers of experienced soldiers available to train and organise the armies being raised by king and Parliament, who competed eagerly for their services. In their turn the veterans were often moti-vated by political sympathies, although some were quite ready to serve whichever employer offered the more favourable terms.

During the summer of 1642 king and Parliament were both faced with the task of raising armies from scratch, each using rather legally questionable means to do so. The king relied initially on Commissions of Array. These were a medieval institution dating back to 1324, but not employed since 1557. Under this legislation, commissioners were appointed by the king in each county, or at least in those where he believed he had significant potential support, with powers to call out all the male population capable of bearing arms. In a similar way, Parlia-ment employed the Militia Ordnance which it had passed, though without royal consent, in

1641. Neither method was calculated to convince waverers, and both sides also issued wealthy or locally influential supporters with commissions to raise regiments. The would-be colonel of such a newly commissioned regiment would usually call on a network of relatives and neighbours to help raise his unit, giving them command of companies of foot or troops of horse which they would then set out to recruit by various means.

In the opening months of the war all regiments theoretically consisted of volunteers, although from the beginning there was always a degree of compulsion involved. Tenants and employees, for example, often had little choice but to follow the dictates of their landlord or master. But, in a land where first-hand experience of the harsh realities of war was limited, there were, in these early days, many who were attracted by the prospects of adventure, the chance to experience new horizons, and by the more mundane prospects of regular pay, clothing and food – and perhaps a goodly share of booty following the expected speedy victory.

Richard Gough, in the Shropshire village of Myddle, remembered seeing as a boy recruiting taking place for the Royalist army mustering at Shrewsbury in September 1642. A commissioner of array, Sir Paul Harris – 'a proud imperious person' – employed two recruiting agents, Robert Moore and Matthew Bagley – 'the veriest knaves in Pimhill hundred'. Gough recounted that

> Harris sent out warrants requiring and commanding all men, both householders with their sons, and servants and sojurnors and others within the hundred of Pimhill that were between the age of sixteen and three score to appear on a certain day upon Myddle Hill … And there I saw a multitude of men, and upon the highest bank of the hill I saw this Robert Moore standing with a paper in his hand, and three or four soldiers' pikes stuck upright in the ground by him, and there he made a proclamation that if any person would serve the King as a soldier in the wars, he should have 14 groats [44p] a week for his pay.[3]

Given that the average wage of an agricultural labourer was 1 groat (3p) a day, this was clearly a very tempting offer. Officers and sergeants also 'beat the drum' for recruits in towns and villages, using the time-honoured methods of plying potential soldiers with strong drink and fair promises.

The majority of recruits thus obtained were, in the case of the Royalists, from agricultural labouring or similar backgrounds. Parliament, by reason of its control of the large towns of southeastern England, tended to attract more urban workers, including London apprentices whose cropped hair led the Royalists to give them the soubriquet 'Roundheads', a description applied, highly inaccurately, to Parliamentarian supporters in general.

In the village of Myddle, Richard Gough listed details of twenty men who joined the Royalist forces. Of these no less than thirteen never returned. Whilst not all will have been fatalities, the figures do suggest a loss rate similar to that of the First World War. Of the twenty recruits, at least seven were unemployed, with criminal records or of no fixed abode. Among them was 'an idle fellow, who was a tailor, and went from place to place in this parish, but had no habitation …' and 'the bastard son of Richard Challinor … This bastard was partly maintained by the parish, and being a big lad, went to Shrewsbury, and was there listed, and went to Edgehill to fight and was never heard of afterwards in this county.'[4]

Parish authorities took the opportunity to off-load assorted undesirables from their local communities, whilst other individuals saw enlistment as a way to escape from various difficulties. Thomas Ash of Myddle was 'a proper comely person with a good country education' but heavily in debt, so he joined up to 'shelter himself from the fatigue of duns'. Men with the ability to read and write were seen as NCO material, and Ash rose to the rank of corporal, but 'brought home nothing but a crazy body and many scars'.[5] There must have been a number of men in Ludlow who enlisted for similar reasons to those which Gough describes.

The failure of the first campaign in the summer and autumn of 1642 to bring about the expected speedy military decision saw the return home in the winter – often as deserters – of some of those eager recruits of the summer, bringing with them tales of the harsh realities of military life. This meant that volunteers became increasingly difficult to obtain. As a result conscription was introduced in Royalist areas in the spring of 1643, and by the end of the year was in general use by both sides.

Decisions on the numbers of recruits required were normally made by the Royalist council of war in Oxford, and by Parliament in London, and quotas to be raised sent to the commissioners of array in Royalist-controlled areas, and to the county committees for those areas in Parliamentarian hands. These recruits were intended, in theory, for the main field armies, and did not necessarily take account of men required in regional and local forces.

The Shropshire Parliamentarians did not have a substantial enough foothold in the county until the latter stages of the war to be able to supply men for more than their own local forces, so impressment in the county was mainly carried out by the Royalists, and would have been entirely so in the case of the Ludlow area. The commissioners of array would have specified a number of men by a stipulated date who, in the case of Shropshire, would have to be mustered at Shrewsbury. The actual conscription process was the responsibility of the civil authorities and carried out by the constables, with military backing if necessary. Sometimes the militia would be mustered and men selected from it, or it might be carried out on a more *ad hoc* basis.

There were, in theory, restrictions on those liable to be conscripted. In 1644, the Carmarthenshire commissioners of array were instructed by the Royalist council of war:

> first for the person you are to imprest for or same you shall make choice- Of such are of able bodyes- Of such as are for their quality fit to be common soldiers- Of such as are fitted by the age between 20 and 60 years- Of such as being single are not housekeepers- Of such as not being housekeepers are out of service rather than such as are in- Of such as are Mechanicks rather than husbandmen.[6]

In practice the constables aimed to rid their local communities of undesirables, and would also endeavour to include any deserters they were able to apprehend, vagrants, and even strangers who were unfortunate enough to be passing through their parish at the wrong moment. Most would have agreed with the guidelines issued by the Parliamentarian High Constable in Norfolk, who instructed his men to 'have an especiall care to take idle serving men and such other able persons who live dissolutely or without imployment'.[7]

On the other hand, the supply of such men was finite, and the army commanders were apt to object to having the dregs of the local community unloaded on them in this way. To add to the local constables' headaches, they were held responsible for the men they pressed until they had been delivered to the military convoy or conductor who was to take them to the army. If the unwilling recruits deserted before this time, as happened in many cases, the constable had to find a substitute. It was not uncommon for a £1 bounty to be offered for any deserter handed over. Though these, in theory, faced the death penalty, they were more usually simply returned to the army, and some evidently deserted, and were re-conscripted, more than once during the war.

The citizens of some towns, for example Chester, were exempted from impressment provided they served in the 'town regiments' raised, in theory, solely for the defence of that place. The situation in Ludlow is unclear. As we shall see, men were raised for the defence of the town, probably under the auspices of the militia or Trained Band, but there is no evidence that the townsmen were exempted from conscription for other units. Certainly some served in Sir Michael Woodhouse's regiment (see chapter 6).

It probably took around two months to produce an adequately trained foot soldier, and a cavalry trooper rather longer. In practice there was rarely this amount of time available and officers had to hope that the draconian punishments available to them would help keep their raw recruits under control. The Royalist 'articles of war', for example, listed thirteen offences punishable by death. They included mutiny, murder, desertion, killing prisoners, and sleeping on guard duty. In the case of common soldiers, execution was normally by hanging. Officers were more usually shot by firing squad. Blasphemy was punishable by the tongue of the guilty party being bored through with a red-hot iron. There were corporal punishments for lesser offences, including running the gauntlet, flogging, and riding the 'wooden horse' – a V-shaped contraption onto which the 'rider' was forced down by weights attached to his feet.[8]

Terrifying though the potential punishments were, in practice there seems to have been a good deal of variation in how they were applied. Deserters were more likely to be forcibly re-conscripted than executed, and most officers took the realistic view that in a situation in which regular pay was an ideal devoutly to be wished for rather than a reality, a certain amount of looting was best tacitly ignored. The penalty for blasphemy was rarely inflicted in the Royalist forces, though more frequently in those of Parliament. In many cases, other than perhaps murder, it appears to have been more usual to carry out the occasional execution as an example, rather than in every case.

Food and Medical Care

The staple food of the lower classes of mid-17th-century society was cheese, beef, or fish, bread and beer. This was reflected in the rations issued to the troops. The daily ration for a common soldier in the Royalist Oxford army consisted of 2lb of bread, 1lb of cheese or meat, and a bottle of wine or two bottles of beer, which compared very well with the average civilian sustenance and has been estimated to provide 4,500 calories, enough for heavy manual labour.[9]

When considering the health of Civil War soldiers, and the medical provision available, it should be remembered that this was a society in which the average life expectancy was no more than 32 years, with 40% of the population aged under 20, and about a third dying before the age of 15. Tuberculosis, dysentery and cholera were among a host of diseases that – to modern eyes – took a horrendous toll, but resulted in early death being a more readily accepted reality than is the case nowadays.

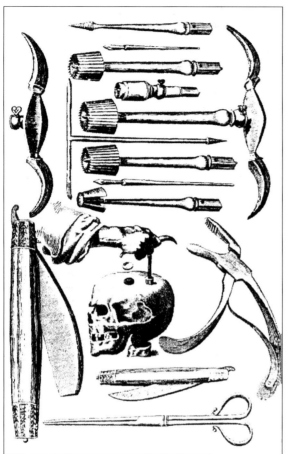

Medical instruments. Many are very similar to their modern counterparts. Although surgery could often be surprisingly effective, lack of knowledge of hygiene resulted in a high mortality rate.

Even so, the Civil War hit hard. Perhaps between 10 and 25% of deaths were the result of combat, the remainder being from disease. The horrific nature of many of the wounds suffered in combat is illustrated in the description by the Parliamentarian chronicler John Vicars of the injuries inflicted by cavalry swords on some unfortunate Royalist infantry: 'most woefully cut and mangled, some having their ears cut off, some the flesh of their heads sheared off, some with their very skull hanging down and ready to fall …'.[10]

Surgeons generally knew how to treat wounds, with instruments remarkably similar to many in use today. Sword cuts, if not infected, usually healed fairly satisfactorily. Gunshot wounds were more problematic, especially as hygiene was imperfectly understood, often resulting in gangrene and often being fatal.

Most regiments endeavoured to have a surgeon, often with two mates, on their establishment, though their ability varied widely. On the battlefield medical care was often overwhelmed by the numbers of casualties, but in a town such as Ludlow, civilian doctors would also be available, and the wounded billeted on townspeople for care.

For those rendered unfit for further service by their wounds, the outlook was often bleak. The king, in theory, made pensions available for Royalist soldiers, but these were rarely paid, and the best hope for a wounded man would be to try to make his way home to the meagre care of his parish poor law overseers.

The Cavalry

Conscription rarely, if ever, seems to have been used to raise cavalry. Not only were recruits generally of a somewhat higher social status than in the foot, possession of a horse would have made desertion a much easier prospect. The cavalry, or 'horse', were regarded as the elite battle-winning force and regiments were therefore normally raised by a commission granted to its colonel. He needed either to be wealthy in his own right, or to have generous benefactors, because apart from incidental costs such as horses and equipment, a troop was estimated to cost around £52 a week to maintain.

Although three-quarter armoured heavy cavalry, or cuirassiers, were occasionally encountered, and the Scots employed lancers, the most usual cavalry in the English Civil War were 'harquebusiers.' These were light or medium horse, equipped with a 'pot' helmet, back and breastplates, or occasionally a hardened leather – or 'buff' – coat, and ideally armed with a short barrelled carbine, a pair of pistols and a sword.

In theory a cavalry regiment consisted of 500 officers and men, organised into roughly six troops, though in practice both the number of troops and their strength varied widely. A regiment was commanded by a colonel, a lieutenant-colonel (in the case of the Royalists) and a major, with each troop having as its commissioned officers a captain, a lieutenant, a cornet and a quartermaster. Each troop was divided into three squadrons commanded by corporals, who were usually experienced soldiers with some basic literacy. A troop in theory had two trumpeters who, as well as conveying orders by their trumpet calls, also acted as messengers, and sometimes as spies. A troop's complement was completed by a clerk, saddler, farrier and ideally, a surgeon and sometimes a chaplain.

A popular misconception about the nature of the opposing cavalry forces has its origins in a well-known comment by Oliver Cromwell made in the aftermath of the Battle of Edgehill in 1642, when he told a fellow Parliamentarian: 'Your troopers are most of them decayed serving men, and tapsters, and such kind of fellows; and their troopers are gentlemen's sons, younger sons and persons of quality.'[11] But even at the beginning of the war this was a sweeping generalisation, and would become even more so in later years, especially among the cavalry units which served along the Welsh border.

In reality the cavalry of both sides, in an age when the majority of the male population were at least adequate riders, was made up from a wide spectrum of society, including the officers. By the later stages of the conflict, the troopers of a typical unit, with little difference between those of king or Parliament, might be roughly one third of gentry background, with the remainder a mixture of yeomen, servants, tenant farmers or indeed anyone able to provide a horse. It was also not unusual for cavalry regiments to include significant numbers

The usual attire of a 'harquebusier', the most common type of cavalry employed in the Civil War. Note the pot helmet and back and breast plates. By the middle of the Civil War, cavalry on both sides were virtually identical in equipment and the tactics they employed.

of foreign mercenaries. John Devalier's Royalist regiment, stationed in and around Ludlow in the later stages of the war, was one such.

Despite the romantic Victorian portrayals of beplumed Cavaliers locked in combat with stern armour-clad 'Ironsides', there was in reality virtually no difference in the arms and equipment of the opposing horse. Nor, from around the middle of 1643 onwards, was there generally much to distinguish them in tactics. The cavalry of both sides advanced to combat at 'a good round trot', at most a gentle canter rather than the full-blooded uncontrollable charge of legend, discharged their pistols, and then engaged with their swords in what might be a prolonged and brutal 'slogging match'.

In the regions the quality of cavalry regiments varied. Some, such as the Royalist Sir William Vaughan's, based on a core of veterans from the war in Ireland, had a fair amount of experience in set-piece actions. Others, particularly units on garrison duty, spent most of their time on foraging raids and small-scale skirmishing.

There is no evidence that most cavalry units, with the possible exception of elite Lifeguard formations, received issues of uniform clothing. This seems to have been left to the individual colonel or troop commander. Officers often favoured scarlet, whilst an ordinary trooper would have a jacket or cassock, breeches, riding boots and a cloak or long riding coat. So far as headwear was concerned, least practical was the broad-brimmed hat of popular legend. Knitted fisherman-style woollen caps were often worn, and were probably especially popular in the Marches, as Bewdley was a noted centre for their manufacture.

The troopers of opposing sides were identified by coloured hat bands or sashes, often red for the Royalists and blue or orange for the Parliamentarians, or by 'field signs', perhaps a flower or sprig of a particular plant. Cavalry standards often bore a political or religious slogan identifying their allegiance, and might or might not have a common regimental pattern.

Most troopers had one horse, initially often provided by themselves on enlistment. If this mount was lost from disease or in battle, they could hope that a replacement would be provided from military sources. These were obtained by purchase from horse dealers, or very often requisitioned, with or without some vague promise of future restoration or financial compensation. Officers might have two or more mounts – a 'riding horse' for everyday use, and a trained horse for battle. As might be expected, obtaining sufficient fodder for the large numbers of horses needed was a constant problem, both for the troopers and for civilian communities on which they were billeted.

Most civil war armies were accompanied by an array of 'camp-followers' of various degrees of legitimacy. Cavalry units often had a number of 'padees' or horse-boys, one being paid or supported by several troopers and tasked with the care of their horses. In November 1645 Sir William Vaughan's force operating in the Marches included a number of padees, some of whom were captured by the Parliamentarians at the Battle of Denbigh Green, but released as being 'not worth the keeping'.[12]

A 17th-century regiment might be accompanied on the march by a surprisingly large number of non-combatants. In 1646 a Bavarian regiment in the Thirty Years' War had 481 troopers, 236 servants, 102 women and children and nine sutlers (civilian merchants who travelled with the regiment, selling goods to its members).[13] The large numbers of civilian camp followers of both sexes who for various motives attached themselves to civil war armies were a frequent source of irritation to commanders.

Maintaining a cavalry regiment was expensive. When they were actually paid, a captain could expect on average 10s a day, a captain 5s, a cornet 4s, and an ordinary trooper 2s. This was one reason that regiments tended to decline in numbers as the war went on, although as their establishment of officers tended to be maintained, however few men they had to command, the costs of upkeep did not decrease in the same proportion.

Although in general the equipment of cavalry troopers improved as the war went on, there were frequently shortages. In late 1645 it was noted of Vaughan's men 'scarce a tenth man hath a pistol'.[14] This may partly have been a result of the common tactic in battle of hurling fired pistols at opponents. In the event of defeat they would not have been recovered.

By the later stages of the war, the Royalist cavalry in the Ludlow area probably resembled a description of Prince Rupert's own troopers following the surrender of Bristol in September 1645:

> First there came a half-dozen of carbines in their leathern coats and starved weather-beaten jades, just like so many brewers in their jerkins made of old boots, riding in to fetch old casks; and after them as many light horsemen with great saddles and scarce a sword amongst them just like so many fiddlers with their fiddles in cases by their horses' sides.[15]

Pikeman. This individual wears full armour of back and breast plates, tassets to protect his thighs, and a morion-style helmet. It is uncertain how much of this armour was regularly worn on campaign.

The Infantry

An infantry – or foot – regiment had a regulation strength of between 1,000 and 1,200 men, plus officers, organised into ten companies of varying sizes, those of the colonel, lieutenant-colonel and major being the largest. A company was commanded by a captain, with a lieutenant, an ensign, and three sergeants, three corporals and two drummers.

The foot were armed with musket and pike, with, in theory, two musketeers for each pikeman. In practice, the ratio varied widely. At the start of the war, when firearms were in short supply, the ratio in Royalist regiments was often 1:1. Later in the war, particularly in garrisons, some regiments were entirely composed of musketeers.

The pike, because of its associations with antiquity, and because pikemen needed to be taller and stronger than musketeers, was still sometimes regarded as the more 'honourable' weapon. A pike was up to 18 feet in length, although frequently shortened by soldiers for greater ease of handling. It had, ideally, an ash pole with a diamond-shaped metal 'spearhead'. Military manuals recommended that pikemen should be issued with a pot helmet and body armour, but, with the possible exception of the helmet, this seems to have rarely been issued or worn, and the dress of most pikemen would have been similar to that of the musketeers.

Infantry were issued with coats or cassocks, ideally of the same colour for the whole regiment, breeches, stockings and

23

shoes, and headwear, with the Montero cap (a peaked cap of various styles made from cloth, often with ear flaps) particularly common among Royalist troops. Although there were a wide variety of coat colours in use, red and blue seem to have been the most common. Woodhouse's Regiment at Ludlow are said to have been 'Bluecoats', though no contemporary source for this assertion has yet been traced. In the opening stages of the war, in regional forces and at the end of a campaigning season, many men wore civilian dress.

This frequent lack of uniformity in dress, with both sides wearing largely identical clothing, meant that confusion and wrong identification was common. Regiments would have individual sets of flags, with a common background colour, not necessarily the same as their coat colour, and bearing a pattern of symbols identifying each individual company in it.

In infantry combat, opposing ranks of pikemen would engage in the tactic known as 'push of

pike', rather like a modern rugby scrum, in which they would attempt to knock over or push back their opponents, though often encounters might amount to not much more than ineffectual 'fencing' with pikes. Their other main role was to act in defence against cavalry when they would form 'hedgehogs', with the musketeers crouched beneath the protecting pikes.

Musketeers normally carried the matchlock musket. This weapon, fired by means of a length of burning match or cord, had an effective range of under a hundred yards. Although military manuals proposed a complicated series of loading and firing movements, in practice on the battlefield simplified methods were used, with a musketeer able to fire around three times a minute.

The matchlock musket had disadvantages. Its firing mechanism could prove unreliable in wet weather, and the lighted match often gave away soldiers' positions at night. But it was a robust weapon, relatively cheap to manufacture, and easy to become accustomed to. Some infantry were equipped with the more sophisticated flintlock or 'firelock'. These were used by specialist units, such as the guards of artillery trains, as they were less likely to result in accidental explosions, which often occurred with the presence of lighted match. The firelock was, however, less reliable, and also more expensive to manufacture.

Musketeer. This soldier is armed with a matchlock musket and sword. Note his bandolier with around a dozen powder chargers, sometimes termed 'apostles', though there is no evidence that this description was used at the time. He carries a musket rest to support his matchlock when firing. The montero cap he is wearing was issued widely to Royalist soldiers.

Pikemen and musketeers also carried cheap swords, used more often for chopping firewood and terrorising civilians than in actual combat. In hand-to-hand mêlées, musketeers normally preferred to reverse their muskets and use them as clubs.

Although the infantry of both sides became better equipped as the war progressed, shortages occurred, especially away from the main manufacturing centres and magazines. Royalist units operating along the Welsh border were often reliant for both arms and powder on munitions from Royalist-held Bristol (after its capture in July 1643), and Parliamentarian interference, especially from troops based at Gloucester, often disrupted transport. In the spring of 1644 it was noted that Prince Rupert's foot on the Welsh border were 'very poor and ragged, very many had no arms but swords'.[16]

Dragoons

A third category of troops were the dragoons. These were basically mounted infantry, armed with a short-barrelled carbine (similar to a musket, but easier to handle on horseback) and sword. They normally rode into battle and then dismounted to fight, often using the cover of hedgerows and walls in a skirmishing role. They were also used for reconnaissance, raids on enemy quarters, foraging and guarding convoys. Dragoons were extensively used in the civil war in Shropshire. Sir Vincent Corbett's regiment was specifically raised by the Royalists for the defence of the county. None seem, however, to have formed part of the Ludlow garrison.

Often associated with dragoons were the firelock units. At least two companies of them formed part of the contingent of English troops from Ireland which was shipped over in the winter of 1643/44 to reinforce the king's armies. In the event most of them were captured at the Battle of Nantwich (25 January 1644) and changed sides, becoming amongst the most effective of the Cheshire Parliamentarian forces. Prince Maurice had a firelock regiment in the southern Welsh Marches in the spring of 1645, and some also served in the garrison of Chirk.

The Artillery

Although of limited significance on the battlefield, artillery was of great importance in siege warfare and garrison defence. There were cannon in the Royalist defences of Ludlow, and in 1646 the Parliamentarian besiegers considered using them, though in the event did not do so. Although there were many lighter pieces, the main types of cannon employed in siege warfare

Artillery. A cannon of the types employed in siege operations. The gun would have had a platform of planks and wickerwork intended to prevent it sinking into the ground from the recoil when it was fired. Note the wicker protective breatswork.

were 12-pounder demi-culverins, 15-pounder culverins, and 27-pounder demi-cannon. They all required a considerable outlay in resources, with crews of between seven and ten men, and needing large teams of horses or oxen to draw them. They were in any case very slow and difficult to transport along the frequently inadequate road system, and water transport was preferred where possible. They also consumed large quantities of frequently scarce gunpowder.

Artillery could however be highly effective against medieval stone fortifications such as those of Ludlow, even if they were backed by a lining of earth, and one consequence was the construction in many garrisons of extensive systems of earth-constructed 'outworks'. These served the dual purposes of protecting the suburbs of towns outside the medieval defences, and keeping besieging artillery further away. They were relatively quick to construct, but often required greater manpower to defend them than was available.

4 War Comes to Ludlow

On 22 August 1642 King Charles I raised his standard at Nottingham. It was the official proclamation of a state of war. Parliament was already mustering a field army under the command of its Lord General, Robert Devereux, Earl of Essex, and across the country activists on both sides were attempting to secure their authority and control of the militia and Trained Bands.

In Herefordshire the local Royalists achieved almost complete, albeit, it would prove, fragile, control. Only Brampton Bryan, in Sir Robert Harley's absence in London left under the determined command of his wife, Lady Brilliana, remained as an island of Parliamentarian territory. Lady Brilliana's frequent letters to her husband expressed her concerns in such an isolated situation. She makes it clear that Ludlow was a hot-bed of rather disorderly Royalist support. On 24 June she informed Sir Robert that townspeople had 'set up a May Pole and a thing like a head on it, and gathered a great many about it and shot at it in derision of roundheads'. She added that 'Every Thursday, some of Ludlow, as they go through the town, wish all the Puritans of Brampton hanged, and as I was walking in the garden, … they looked upon me and wished all the Puritans and Roundheads at Brampton hanged …'.[1]

However, these disorderly characters did not have everything their own way; Lady Brilliana went on to describe how William Littleton, a Puritan from Bishop's Castle 'being in Ludlow last week, as he came out of the church, a man came to him and looked him in the face and cried "roundhead!"; he gave the fellow a good box of the ear and stepped to one that had a cudgel and took it from him and beat him soundly'.[2]

This loud-mouthed royalism did not at this stage translate into much practical action so far as Shropshire, including presumably

Lady Brilliana Harley (1600?-43). A lady of strong puritan beliefs, Brilliana was among a number of women who found themselves, at least nominally, in command of the defence of their family homes during the war.

Ludlow, was concerned. The king's Commission of Array, calling for the enlistment of the county militia, reached the High Sheriff of Shropshire, John Weld, at Shrewsbury on 24 July. Weld and the other named commissioners of array called a muster of the militia at Shrewsbury for 4 August. However, Parliamentarian supporters attempted to pre-empt this by calling their own muster for the previous day. The Mayor intervened, threatening to arrest those who appeared, and with Royalist supporters also arriving on the scene, a riot nearly ensued.

Both parties attempted to begin drilling recruits over the next few days, but attempts to gain wider support in the county foundered in the face of indifference or active hostility. The Royalist commissioners – headed by Francis Ottley, Sir Paul Harris, and Sir Vincent Corbet – had met at Much Wenlock on 3 August and urged the Shropshire gentry to join them, purportedly in order to preserve the 'peace' of the county. Their call had been met with an unenthusiastic response.

The situation was transformed by the decision of King Charles, following the disappointing response he met after raising his standard at Nottingham, to move to Shrewsbury. Here he could draw in recruits from predominantly Royalist north Wales and the Earl of Derby's estates in Lancashire and Cheshire, as well as from along the Welsh border. The king arrived in Shrewsbury, which by this time had been secured for the Royalist cause by John Weld and Francis Ottley, on 17 September, and summoned the gentry to meet him there on 28 September. A message was also sent to the bailiffs of Ludlow, among others, ordering the horse and foot of the Trained Band 'to appear before His Majesty at Shrewsbury' on 29 September.[3]

The war was by now coming uncomfortably closer to Ludlow. The king had sent a regiment of horse under Sir John Byron to secure the plate and other valuable of the University of Oxford to help finance his war effort. Having carried out the first part of his mission, Byron headed for Worcester, with the Parliamentarian army of the Earl of Essex heading in the same direction. Byron was almost caught at Worcester by Essex's advance guard, but rescued by Prince Rupert, the king's nephew and General of Horse, in a brisk little action outside the city at Powicke Bridge on 23 September. Byron and Rupert then headed for Shrewsbury, taking the university plate with them, by way of Tenbury Wells. Rupert seems to have left cavalry outposts in the vicinity to observe the movements of Essex's army, now in occupation of Worcester.

Parliamentarian newsletters – propaganda being an area in which for the moment the king's opponents were virtually uncontested – began laying claims to a series of victories over the 'Cavaliers'. One such victory was alleged to have occurred near Ludlow. According to an account in a pamphlet entitled *True Intelligence and Joyful News From Ludlow*, Essex's army followed Rupert from Worcester in order to avenge the defeat at Powicke Bridge, and had defeated him on 1 October at 'Standard Oak', following a 'great charge'. There is a 'Standard Oak' between Mortimer's Cross and Ludford, but a more likely location would have been 'Stanton Oak', halfway between Ludlow and Tenbury Wells. According to *True Intelligence*, the Parliamentarians followed up their victory by advancing on Ludlow, and taking the heavily defended castle after a seven-hour battle.

The alleged 'Battle of Standard Oak' was accepted as an actual event by some later writers, but such a battle never took place. Essex would have sent cavalry patrols probing out from Worcester, but his main army did not march any further westwards. As for Rupert, *The Journal of Prince Rupert's Marches,* an almost daily record of his movements during the civil war probably compiled by his secretary, records for 25 September: 'Sunday, to Ludlow Castle, a false alarm'. The following day Rupert continued northwards to Haughmond, north-east of Shrewsbury, and was then involved with the training and mustering of recruits at Shrewsbury, with no mention of a return to Ludlow, or any contact with the Parliamentarian army.[4] The most that can have happened is a skirmish between cavalry patrols, and Ludlow certainly did not come under attack, or Parliamentarian occupation.

Although the Ludlow Trained Bands, probably totalling one company of about 100 men, had been ordered to the muster at Shrewsbury, in order that a selection of men could be made as 'volunteers' (in effect conscripted) for the army which the king was mustering, it seems that the response was by no means whole-hearted. On 5 December the bailiffs at Ludlow received another letter from the commissioners of array in Shrewsbury, in which they complained that many of those for whom warrants had been sent to muster at Shrewsbury had 'neither sent their horse, nor show reason for their neglect'. They were to answer the renewed summons and be at Shrewsbury by 15 December 'by nine of the clock in the morning there to be mustered by us otherwise their names shall be returned to his Majesty as disaffected members to his service'. Those who had already answered the summons were thanked, and were to muster as arranged, 'to be delivered to the Captain and also exercised by him'.[5]

The men of Ludlow were not alone in this evident reluctance to serve. Throughout the country that autumn people clung to the hope that the war would be settled by the result of one decisive battle, and that they would be spared further involvement. At this stage no full regiments were raised in Shropshire, though it may be that Ludlow men served in the units originally raised in north Wales and elsewhere and filled out during the king's stay at Shrewsbury.

The Royalist army left Shrewsbury on 13 October on the first stage of its march on London. The anticipated encounter with the Parliamentarian army of the Earl of Essex took place on 23 October at Edgehill in Warwickshire. A fiercely fought engagement ended in a narrow Royalist victory, but the king's advance on London faltered when his advance was blocked on the outskirts of the capital at Turnham Green in November. Charles established a temporary capital at Oxford, and the armies went into winter quarters.

When the Earl of Essex marched to intercept King Charles, he left garrisons in Worcester and Hereford. However, surrounded by predominantly Royalist territory, neither garrison could do more than carry out minor raids on their immediate neighbourhoods. The Parliamentarians evacuated Hereford in November and Worcester in the following month, and, with the exception of Lady Brilliana Harley in her isolated stronghold at Brampton Bryan, Ludlow had no Parliamentarian troops near at hand.

There was indeed no effective Parliamentarian presence in Shropshire as 1643 dawned. None of the leading landowners actively supported Parliament, and until Wem was occupied later in the spring, the Parliamentarians had no Shropshire base of operations. Throughout the war they had little military success unless the bulk of Royalist forces were operating elsewhere. In February 1643, in opposition to the Royalist commissioners of array, Parliament established, as elsewhere, a Shropshire county committee including among its membership Thomas Hunt, a Shrewsbury lawyer, Humphrey Mackworth, Thomas Mytton of Halston and Andrew Lloyd of Aston. But it was not until September that it was able to establish a Shropshire foothold at Wem.

Whether through lack of zest for the Royalist cause, or lack of a local Parliamentarian 'threat', during the winter of 1642-43 the Royalists continued to encounter widespread apathy in Shropshire. In December it was proposed to raise a regiment of dragoons, under Sir Vincent Corbet, paid for by subscriptions from 33 Shropshire gentry, tasked with the defence of the county. A levy for its maintenance was to be raised by levels fixed at meetings held in each hundred, but the response was disappointing. Sir Thomas Scriven, one of the commissioners of array, was more than a little annoyed in a summons to the constable of Purslow Hundred despatched on 10 January. Having had no response to several warrants requiring the collection of payments to maintain troops, he ordered all the militia of the hundred to muster at Ludlow on a stipulated day 'by nine in the morning with their arms complete, and that gentlemen and other inhabitants of the hundred who are contributors to maintenance also to be there, to see them well furnished and to satisfy me and others why their money were not sent in according to warrants'.[6]

This suggests that the majority of communities were essentially focused on local considerations. Bishop's Castle corporation, for example, set up its own local defence force, based on its Trained Band, to protect itself against unspecified marauders.

The spring, however, saw the threat of Parliamentarian attack on Ludlow increasing. The year began with Brampton Bryan the only pocket of Parliamentarian territory in the vicinity of Ludlow, but half-hearted attempts by the Herefordshire Royalists to blockade Lady Brilliana into surrender proved ineffective.

Lord Arthur Capel (1610-49). An Essex man, Capel was probably appointed as Royalist commander in the northern Welsh Marches because of the lack of an obvious local figure for the role. Partly because of a lack of troops and resources and partly due to local apathy, but also through his own indifferent generalship, Capel proved unsuccessful.

In March a Parliamentarian army under Sir William Waller arrived at Gloucester, and forced the surrender of Lord Herbert's newly raised army from south Wales at Highnam. This was followed on 25 April by the collapse of the Herefordshire Royalists and the surrender of Hereford to Waller almost without resistance. Fortunately for Royalist Ludlow, Waller made no attempt to advance any further, and indeed felt his position at Hereford to be too exposed to maintain. In early May he retreated southwards, eventually back to Gloucester, and the pressure was for the moment eased.

In March, in an effort to revitalise the Royalist war effort in Shropshire and the northern marches, King Charles appointed Arthur, Lord Capel, as Lieutenant General in command in the area, with his headquarters at Shrewsbury. Capel, with extensive estates in Essex and Hertfordshire, was a dedicated Royalist of high social status. His military experience was limited however, and it was probably because of this that Capel brought Michael Woodhouse with him to Shropshire, a man who would be of key importance in Ludlow's role in the war.

Woodhouse was born in Leiden in the Netherlands in 1601, the eldest son of Captain Henry Woodhouse, a Norfolk man who was evidently a professional soldier probably serving with the English regiments in Dutch service against Spain. Henry Woodhouse's wife, Judith was probably Dutch. By 1610 the family had returned to Winterton in Norfolk, where Michael's younger sisters were born, and where his father died in 1637. Michael Woodhouse followed in his father's footsteps as a professional soldier. In 1634 he was with the Earl of Hamilton's unsuccessful expedition to Germany, serving as a 'page' or adjutant to the earl. The outbreak of the rebellion in Ireland gave Woodhouse opportunity for employment nearer to home, and he was Major to the notorious Richard Grenvile in the English garrison of Trim, which had a fearsome reputation for brutality.[7]

Woodhouse evidently returned to England during the winter of 1642/3, probably making his way to Royalist Oxford, where he was appointed Major-General of Foot to Lord Capel, and commissioned to raise a regiment of foot himself. The Prince of Wales Regiment of Foot, as it was termed, was raised initially mainly in the Denbigh area of north Wales, although further recruits were added from central Wales and Shropshire. It is sometimes asserted that Woodhouse's regiment was 'Irish', but whilst it is likely that some of its officers were English or Welsh who had served in Ireland, there is nothing to suggest that any of its rank and file were English troops who had served there, still less 'native' Irish.[8] As noted earlier, Woodhouse's regiment was known as 'bluecoats', indicating that they were issued with blue coats, although evidence of this has not yet been found.

Sir Francis Ottley (1601-49). Pictured here with his family, Ottley was Governor of Shrewsbury in 1642-43. Ottley was the most active Royalist in the town, though he fell out of favour with Prince Rupert and was replaced early in 1644.

On 16 April Woodhouse wrote to Francis Ottley in Shrewsbury, thanking him for two experienced sergeants he had supplied for the new regiment, and asking that some soldiers be put in their care. He hoped that another 60 recruits would be delivered to his Major by Sir Thomas Salisbury, a leading Royalist from the Denbigh area of north Wales who had previously raised his own regiment which had fought at Edgehill.[9]

Capel was seriously short of troops, though weaponry was less of a problem as the iron foundries at Bouldon and Coalbrookdale were producing both muskets and cannon using the iron ore mined in the Clee Hills and Coalbrookdale. For the moment military operations were confined to the borders of Shropshire and Cheshire, where indecisive skirmishing with the Cheshire Parliamentarian forces of Sir William Brereton continued through the spring and early summer.

In Ludlow there were clear signs that the town was being put on a war footing. On 31 May Ottley at Shrewsbury received a letter from Thomas Fisher, who described himself as Ludlow's Governor. The Fishers of Dodmore were a prominent burgess family – Richard Fisher had been a bailiff in the 1630s. Although it is not clear if Thomas was a council member, it is very likely that he was. It may be that he had links with the Trained Band causing him to be chosen to take charge of Ludlow's defence, although he does not appear to have received any formal recognition as 'governor' by the king. Certainly, he would be granted a lease by the corporation of 'the Hills', a 40-acre estate near his home, 'in consideration of his love and faithful preservation of this town in the time of hostilities',[10] and an otherwise undated entry in the churchwarden's

A section of Ludlow's town walls.

accounts confirms that Fisher was acting as governor: 'Paid for ringing at two severall days by the apt of Mr Fisher then Governor 3s 4d.'[11]

The Parliamentarians later alleged that Fisher brought cannon from Bringewood Forge, operated by Francis Walker of Wooton and Clungunford, to Ludlow to strengthen its defences and to have raised a company of foot in the town. This was probably based on the Trained Band, and intended purely for the defence of the town. There is also evidence that at some stage a powder mill was operating in Ludlow without which in the later stages of the war any cannon may have been useless.[12]

The town was in a naturally strong defensive position. On the north side a steep escarpment facing the confluence of the Rivers Teme and Corve provided a natural base for the wall constructed on its crest. On the south side of the ridge the River Teme offered a natural barrier, backed again by the town wall. Ludlow's defences also included the castle, although that was self-contained, and under royal, not municipal control. The most vulnerable approaches were to the east and north-east.

Construction of Ludlow's walls began around 1233, and seems to have climaxed in the 1260s. Constructed from local stone, and a mile in circumference, the crenellated walls had seven principal gates. Outside the walls was a dry ditch, about 23 feet wide and 10 feet deep. The main gates – Old Gate, Broad Gate and probably Galdeford Gate and Corve Gate – had twin drum towers and probably drawbridges, and in the case of Broad Gate at least, a port-

Broad Gate. Note the twin drum towers which were a feature of all four of Ludlow's main town gates. The later extension at the front left of the gate, and the Wheatsheaf Inn on the right, occupy the site of the dry ditch which still existed during the Civil War.

View of Ludlow Castle in 1684, from Whitcliffe Common looking over Dinham Bridge.
Note that the castle remained substantially intact. A section of town wall can be seen to the right,
extending down to Dinham Gate.

cullis. There was a dungeon at the base of the eastern of its pair of towers which was probably used as an 'overflow' prison during the Civil War. The lesser gateways were not as imposing, probably lacking portcullis and drawbridge. The gates themselves were made of timber and double-leafed.

Although none of the surviving illustrations confirm its presence, there was almost certainly a wall walk running the length of the town walls. There also seem to have been an uncertain number of D-shaped towers at intervals along the walls.[13]

The earliest detailed panorama of Ludlow, dated 1725, depicts the wall on the south and western sides of Ludlow as still being substantially complete – apart possibly from some breaches

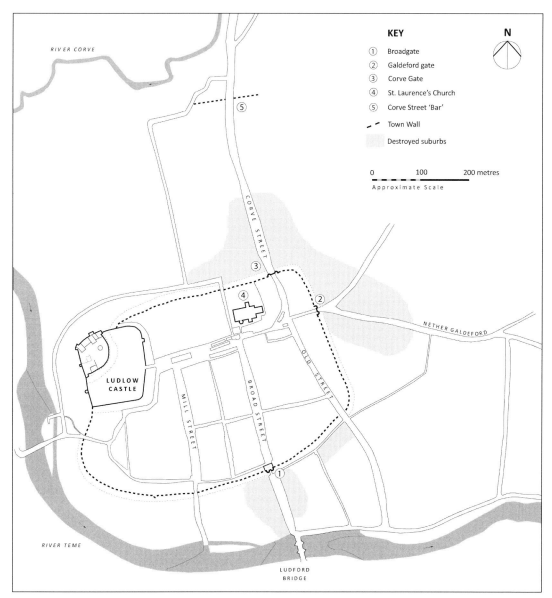

Plan of Ludlow showing the town walls and other features, together wiith the areas of the suburbs later cleared to prevent their use by an enemy force besieging the town (see pages 86-86).

near Dinham Gate – and crenellated, an impression supported by Dinley's 1684 sketches of the neighbourhood of the castle.

As was the case with most English towns, the maintenance of Ludlow's medieval defences had no doubt been lacklustre since the Wars of the Roses, since when the country had been largely peaceful. Because of Ludlow's continued significance as the headquarters of the Council in the Marches, the walls may have been better maintained than some, and certainly there is evidence that at least some repairs were carried out during the 16th century. The bailiff's accounts of 1576/7 and 1624/5, for example, record payments for repairs to the town walls where they adjoined the churchyard.[14]

The castle was in much better repair than many of its counterparts as a result of its occupation by the Council in the Marches. Much of it, including the Judge's Lodgings, was habitable, and probably required minimal refurbishment. There was no garrison at the beginning of the war, when it seems likely that it had no more than a small care and maintenance staff, headed by the constable or porter.[15]

The suburbs of Ludlow, Lower Broad Street and Lower Corve Street along with the southern ends of Mill Street and Old Street, and most of Galdeford to the east, had never been within the medieval defences, and so were vulnerable to attack. There was only a small moveable barrier, or turnpike, termed a "bar", on Lower Corve Street. Evidently Thomas Fisher and the corporation took steps in the spring of 1643 to extend and strengthen the town defences, as confirmed in the Council Minutes of May, when all the inhabitants were ordered to help construct a defensive ditch and earth 'wall' at the foot of their gardens by Whitsuntide, or pay a fine of 10s.[16] It is rather unclear what was meant by this. Plainly there would have been no military purpose to such work in every garden. Presumably the intention was to construct earth outworks at vulnerable points in probably Corve Street, Galdeford and Lower Broad Street, very possibly covering the approaches to Ludford and Corve Bridges. It may be that earthen defences were constructed, or planned, more generally on the Galdeford and Corve Street approaches to the town, but no traces of any such work have been found to give any clearer idea. It would in any case have been impracticable for Ludlow's available manpower to defend an extensive defence line.

Located as it was in a reasonably securely held Royalist area, Ludlow Castle was felt to be a suitable location to hold important prisoners. On 5 June, Sir Nicholas Byron, Colonel General and second-in-command to Lord Capel, wrote to 'the Keeper of Prisoners' at Ludlow, committing to his charge five prisoners from Beaumaris 'which place, in respect of the Situation thereof, is subject to danger [of attack from the sea], and it therefore thought fit that they be removed from thence'.[17]

The prisoners were George Dodding (later a Parliamentarian colonel), Ralph Adams, Francis Fitzhugh, George Tolson and Robert Bradshaw, 'then in actual rebellion against His Majesty'. A letter of 10 June from Sir Richard Lloyd, Governor of Holt Castle, informed 'the Constable of the Castle, Porter of the Lodge, and Keeper of the Gaol' that the prisoners were to be detained 'until they be thence delivered by due Course of Law', the intention being that they might be suitable to be exchanged for Royalists in Parliamentarian custody. They were despatched in the custody of seven guards, who were to receive additional escort from Royalist forces on their route.[18]

Sir William Waller's presence in Hereford may have heightened fears in Ludlow. Indeed, Lord Capel admitted that Waller's presence 'gave this country a great alarm and drew a good part of my men to regard Ludlow'. However, with Waller's departure from the region, the early summer of 1643 was a fairly quiet time for Ludlow. In April, even with Woodhouse's regiment still not complete, Capel was able to say that 'all at Ludlow is now so quiet' and he withdrew his forces from the area for more active operations in north Shropshire.[19]

At Brampton Bryan Lady Brilliana Harley had passed a fairly quiet winter. The Parliamentarian outpost was regarded by the Herefordshire Royalists as a dangerous centre of disaffection, and also a threat to their line of communications along the Welsh border. Partly because of Waller's incursion into the region, there was no immediate move against Brampton Bryan, other than a campaign of intimidation against the Harley tenants in an effort to prevent them from paying their rents. Horses and cattle were driven off the estates and the Harley servants mishandled.

Even after Waller's departure there was no immediate apparent enthusiasm by the local Royalists to take decisive action. However the Royalists in Herefordshire now had a new leader in Sir Henry Lingen, acting under the recently appointed Sir William Vavasour, who was, as Colonel General in Herefordshire, Gloucestershire and Worcestershire, himself theoretically subordinate to Lord Herbert in south Wales. This caused Lady Harley to consider that moves would soon be made against her, and so she began to prepare for the expected attack, strengthening the defences of Brampton Bryan Castle and reinforcing the garrison, whilst her men launched raids into the neighbouring countryside to bring in provisions.

By the middle of July, despite continuing local apathy, Vavasour had raised a force of 1,200 foot and about 200 horse, reinforced by about 700 Herefordshire troops under Lingen, and although his main concern was with Parliamentarian-held Gloucester, he felt that a move against Brampton Bryan would be good for local Royalist morale. Brampton Bryan had a garrison of around just 50 men.

Brampton Bryan Castle By 1642 a fortified residence, Brampton Bryan proved a persistent irritant to the Ludlow Royalists. Its defenders withstood a rather half-hearted Royalist siege in the summer of 1643, before succumbing to a more sustained attack in April 1644.

Operations began on 26 July, when livestock in the vicinity were driven off by the Royalists and the village of Brampton Bryan largely destroyed. However the siege was not pressed with any great vigour. Vavasour lacked the heavy guns necessary to breach the castle walls, and early in August he withdrew his own troops to reinforce the king's army besieging Gloucester. Lingen was left in command at Brampton Bryan, but even though he had now been provided with a demi-culverin which might have made some impact on the castle defences, he too did not press the siege with vigour. His bombardments were spasmodic, perhaps because, with Royalist resources concentrated on the operations at Gloucester, he may have been short of ammunition. Lady Brilliana made skilful use of the apparent reluctance of her near neighbours and pre-war acquaintances to act aggressively, by playing for time in a series of parleys and messages to the king, and on 9 September the siege was abandoned. Lady Harley, already ill in the closing stages of the siege, did not live long to enjoy her success, dying suddenly of pleurisy in October. Command of the garrison, and responsibility for her children there, passed to Dr Nathaniel Wright.[20]

Meanwhile, Lord Capel had been suffering a series of setbacks. Short of both men and munitions, and leaving Woodhouse and his regiment to hold Whitchurch, Capel made a half-hearted attack on Sir William Brereton's base at Nantwich, but was outmanoeuvred by the Parliamentarian commander, who in turn chased Woodhouse's raw recruits out of Whitchurch and plundered the town. A further Royalist assault on Nantwich in July met with another sound repulse, and Capel was forced onto the defensive, making further demands for money and men on the reluctant towns and gentry of Shropshire.

On 9 September the Parliamentarians established what was to prove to be a permanent foothold in Shropshire when they occupied and began fortifying the town of Wem. Capel for the moment could do little to prevent them, as he had been ordered to detach Woodhouse's regiment, still below strength with 700 men, and that of Colonel Richard Herbert, to reinforce the king's main army for the campaign which culminated in the drawn First Battle of Newbury (20 September). Woodhouse and his men were in the thick of the fighting, with Woodhouse knighted for gallantry, but his regiment suffering heavy losses in killed and wounded: 69 common soldiers, 2 captains, 2 lieutenants, 1 ensign and 1 sergeant; roughly 10% of the regiment's strength.[21]

During these campaigns Thomas Fisher was still probably acting as Governor of Ludlow, though, in a sign of tightening military control,

Sir William Brereton (1604-61), Parliamentarian commander in Cheshire from early 1643. A better administrator than commander in battle, Brereton was accused of cowardice on at least one occasion. His qualities of dogged determination, however, helped bring success in his long blockade of Chester.

it seems that the castle was for a time commanded by a professional soldier from Capel's army, Lieutenant-Colonel John Marrow.[22]

Following the First Battle of Newbury, Herbert's and Woodhouse's regiments were returned to Capel's command. Both were re-equipped before they left the king's army, as a series of documents in the Royalist Ordnance Papers describe. On 28 September, Henry Lord Percy, Royalist General of the Ordnance instructed his Lieutenant-General, Sir John Heydon:

> You are forthwith upon sight hereof to issue out of his Majesty's Magazine ten barrels of powder ten barrels of bullet and twenty hundred weight of match. And the same to send away to the town of Woodstock, and there to deliver it to Colonel Woodhouse or such as he shall appoint to receive the same. Court at Oxford the 28th of September 1643.

Woodhouse duly signed for the powder and match, as well as 10 hundredweight of musket shot.

A similar instruction was issued on behalf of Herbert's regiment, though the supplies signed for were exactly half the amounts issued to Woodhouse; Herbert's regiment had been less heavily involved in the fighting at Newbury and had lost just thirteen men. However he was also provided with 150 muskets, with the proviso that they would be returned 'to His Majesty's stores in specie by the first of March next'.

Instructions were also issued as to the departure of the regiments:

> The Conductors who go with the Ammunition for Sir Michael Woodhouse and Colonel Herbert are to march to Aynstone five miles beyond Woodstock in the road to Worcester, they are to send back the Artillery Horses, to Oxford, and provide fresh teams for the Carriages One Conductor going along, unless Colonel Woodhouse consign the Ammunition to some Officer of his own. Five Barrels of Powder and 1000 lb of Match and 500 weight of Bullets are for Colonel Herbert, the rest for Sir Michael Woodhouse. Oxford September 28th, 1643.

The ammunition and arms under the care of Robert Horne, 'Conductor', reached Ludlow Castle safely on 12 October 1643.[23]

By 2 October Woodhouse himself was in Worcester, from where he wrote disapprovingly of the confused state of affairs in Shropshire. He and his regiment continued north to re-join Capel.[24] Richard Herbert and his regiment, however, were despatched to Ludlow, the regiment as garrison and Herbert as Governor, with effect from 28 September.

Born in 1600, Richard Herbert was the eldest son of Edward Lord Herbert of Chirbury, the eccentric scholar, patron of the arts and leading border landowner, who had his seat at Montgomery Castle. Unlike his somewhat politically equivocal father, Richard was a leading supporter of King Charles. He was married to Mary, daughter of the Earl of Bridgewater, Lord President of the Council in the Marches, and had been a strong supporter of Archbishop Laud. As an MP in both the Short Parliament of 1640 and the Long Parliament of the following year, Herbert took the rash step of speaking in favour of Ship Money – though he was forced to retract! He served, with such distinction as was possible in such an ill-managed affair, in the Bishops' War of 1640, and in 1642 was appointed as a commissioner of array in Shropshire,

Montgomeryshire and Monmouthshire, himself commissioned to raise a regiment of foot for which the men were mainly drawn, at least initially, from the Herbert estates around Montgomery. Recruiting had begun by 13 September, but Herbert's regiment was not completed in time to take part in the Edgehill campaign, so served as the garrison of Bridgnorth until the spring of 1643, when it joined the army at Oxford, seeing action at the bloody storming of Bristol in July and the siege of Gloucester.[25]

Herbert now took up residence in Ludlow Castle, where his magazine of ammunition was also housed, whilst some of his men were billeted on the townspeople. The decision to garrison Ludlow with experienced troops reflected both the increasing significance of the town to the Royalists and also their deteriorating position in Shropshire.

In the middle of October Capel, reinforced by Woodhouse's regiment and other troops so that he had a total strength of around 3,000 men, made renewed attacks on Nantwich and Wem. Both were repulsed with heavy loss, and Capel, an object of derision now to both friend and foe, retreated to Shrewsbury. The Parliamentarians were able to strengthen their grip in northern Shropshire and mount an invasion of north-east Wales. Though for the moment Ludlow was not threatened, the outlook was becoming ominous.

There are few references to Herbert's time as Governor of Ludlow. He seems, judging by a complaint he made to Prince Rupert in January 1644,[26] to have had problems in obtaining money and supplies from the Shropshire commissioners of array, who were no doubt preoccupied by the situation in the north of the county. Nor is there evidence of his relationship with the townspeople and corporation. Both seem generally to have been fairly subservient to the military governors of the town, but there are none of the complaints which were to surface fairly regularly when Sir Michael Woodhouse was Governor. This may be because Richard Herbert was only Governor for a short time, or it may be that as his regiment had been raised fairly close by, there was a better rapport between soldiers and civilians in the town.

The available evidence suggest that the system of 'free quarter', by which householders fed the troops billeted on them at a stipulated rate and were recompensed on the presentation of bills, or 'billets', to the military authorities, appears to have functioned satisfactorily during Herbert's time in Ludlow. An item in the bailiff's accounts, referring to several soldiers billeted in one house at a stipulated rate per man, indicates thast payment was duly made:

> For billeting of Richard Herbert's soldiers from the 25th of October 1643 for 10 weeks at 3s 1d per week £52 10s 0d.[27]

But the harsh reality of war was about to be felt much closer to home.

5   HOPTON 'MASSACRE'

In November 1643 the war in the Welsh Marches entered a new more bitter phase with the landing at Mostyn in north Wales of the first detachments of troops from the English forces in Ireland, released for use in England by the 'cessation' or truce which had been reached between King Charles and the Irish rebels known as the Confederates. The newcomers were tough veterans, hard-bitten and ruthless, and they brought with them the harsh methods of the war in Ireland.

Lord Capel was already discredited at the Court in Oxford as a result of his lack of success and Lord Byron was temporarily placed in command of the forces from Ireland, while, on 6 January 1644, Prince Rupert was appointed as Captain General of Wales and the Marches. Aged 23, Rupert, as King Charles' nephew, had been appointed as General of Horse on the outbreak of the Civil War. His previous military experience had been limited, and there were more experienced soldiers who resented an appointment which they felt owed more to dynastic connections than to proven ability. Nonetheless, the prince is generally credited with being the driving force in the creation of the formidable Royalist cavalry which won a string of sweeping successes in the opening year of the war.

Rupert is usually regarded as being one of the great 'romantic' figures of English history, a dashing 'beau sabreur'. The reality was more complicated. Harsh and confrontational by nature, with none of the love of good living enjoyed by many of his colleagues, the prince frequently found himself at odds and ill at ease in the refined circles of the royal court. Indeed it was largely the support and favour of his uncle, King Charles, which enabled him to maintain his position. Although Rupert would prove to have limitations in the role of an army commander, he was nevertheless an able administrator. He had, however, little sympathy for the impact of war on civilians, and throughout his career was linked to actions which in many contemporary eyes stretched the sometimes ill-defined 'laws of war' beyond breaking point, such as the sack of Birmingham in 1643 and the 'Bolton Massacre' in the following year.

Rupert was bombarded with complaints regarding Capel's chaotic administration from the professional soldiers in the area even before he assumed his new command. Woodhouse and another experienced commander, Sir John Mennes, were sent in advance to Shrewsbury to assess the situation. They were unimpressed; on 9 February Woodhouse told Rupert that guard duty was neglected by the inhabitants, and that he had ordered that in future 30 of his own men should stand sentry along with the same number of townsmen.[1] Mennes and Woodhouse caused uproar by hanging a sentry caught sleeping on duty and threatening to do the same to the town marshal for allowing a prisoner to escape. Mennes snarled in a letter to the prince

Prince Rupert (1619-82) (National Portrait Gallery).
In reality Rupert was not entirely the romantic figure of legend.
He was both ruthless and abrasive, though an effective administrator and cavalry commander.

about 'the insulting people, who now tell us their power, and that three of the commissioners of array may question the best of us, from which power good Lord deliver me'.[2]

Pausing to install another professional soldier, Sir Lewis Kirke, as Governor of Bridgnorth, Rupert reached Shrewsbury on 19 February, from where he ordered a large-scale reorganisation of Royalist finances in the area. There was to be a county levy of 6d in the pound on all men's estates, 'without partiality or excuse'.[3] The bailiffs at Ludlow were informed of the new arrangements:

> Prince Rupert Count Palatine of the Rhine Duke of Bavaria and Cumberland, Earl of Holderness Knight of the most noble Order of the Garter General of all his Majesty's horse forces whatsoever and General of the Counties of Worcestershire, Salop, Chester, Lancaster and the six counties of North Wales
>
> To the Worshipful the Bailiffs of the town and liberties of Ludlow
>
> The great inequality heretofore used in the assessing and collecting the payments of this County coming to our notion and knowledge occasioneth us to endeavour the prevention of having any payments or money raised for his majesty's service by our command in that unequal way and to have the same done with as much justice as we can devise or you expect which we doubt not but will be effected if you and the country will not be wanting to yourselves, for which purpose we have appointed certain Commissioners together with yourselves to cause that proportion of the sum of £6000 which is to be paid out of your town and liberties by information upon oath, to be duly and indifferently taxed upon the several inhabitants of the said town and liberties thereof, and for the better proceeding therein and to the intent that the said assessment may be made with all possible indifference. These are therefore to command you that forthwith upon receipt hereof you cause speedy notice and warning to be given to 20 of the most substantial honest men of the best integrity and knowledge of the estates and condition of every one of the inhabitants within every ward or division within the said town and liberties thereof to appear before yourselves and the rest of the said Commissioners in the town hall of Ludlow upon Saturday the second of March by nine of the clock in the forenoon to the intent that a convenient number of the fittest of them may be chosen out of every ward or division within your said town and liberties to assist you and the said commissioners by information upon their oaths for the taxing and assessing of the several inhabitants of your said town and liberties justly truly and indifferently according to their estates and condition further we require you for the better information of yourselves and our said Commissioners in the business that you have ready in writing fairly written the said day and place the names of every inhabitant of your said town and liberties, every particular ward hamlet, village and township by itself. Fail not in the full and punctual performance hereof as you and either of you will answer the contrary at your utmost peril. Given under our hand and seal the 24th day of February 1643 [1644 in the modern calendar]
>
> You are to take notice that if there be any failing in the performance of what is hereby required then we shall immediately levy the sum of your town and liberties required of some of the most sufficient inhabitants of the same in a full double proportion in respect of their contempt.
>
> Rupert.[4]

This uncompromising command and latent threat in the final paragraph must have been viewed in Ludlow with dismay, and it was only the beginning of a turbulent time. The Royalist position in the Marches had been seriously threatened by the defeat suffered by the troops from Ireland commanded by Lord Byron at Nantwich on 25 January. But further reinforcements from the English army in Ireland had now arrived, and enabled Rupert and his commanders to begin active operations to recover lost ground and reduce a number of Parliamentarian garrisons.

It was inevitable that their attention should turn towards the enclave centred on Brampton Bryan. The Parliamentarian garrison in the castle had been left largely undisturbed for some months, but Dr Wright, together with Samuel More, the most active supporter of Parliament in south-west Shropshire, learnt of Royalist plans to garrison Hopton Castle six miles north-west of Ludlow in order to hinder raids from Brampton Bryan, and resolved to pre-empt them.

Hopton Castle probably had 13th-century origins, but hitherto had had an uneventful history. It seems that much of the medieval castle and its defences had already been demolished, or had fallen into ruin, and that what remained consisted principally of the inner bailey, with a curtain wall and attached buildings, along with the Great Tower, which may have been 15th-century in origin, and was of two storeys, with a single room on each. There was apparently some form of moat, or at least marshy ground, around the outside of the inner ward. Hopton Castle was owned by another Parliamentarian sympathiser, Henry Wallop, currently absent.[5]

In the event, the Ludlow forces were ahead of More and were first to establish a garrison at Hopton. More was not deterred, however, and on 18 February, as a Parliamentarian officer related:

Hopton Castle. 13th century in origin, the castle had an uneventful history until the outbreak of the Civil War. The Great Tower (pictured here) was the final refuge of the defenders, who fought to hold its doorway. What remained of the curtain wall before the start of the siege is unkown.

> In the beginning of the night our men came to the gate [of Hopton Castle], one knocked, a soldier within demanded who was there? One of ours replied. 'Here is one, what do you not know me?' 'Who, John Lane?' quoth he ' yes, the very same', whereupon he immediately opened the gate, and our men possessed themselves of the Castle.[6]

The news of the loss of Hopton Castle caused considerable annoyance to the Royalists. It seems that Sir Michael Woodhouse and his regiment had already been sent to Ludlow by Prince Rupert in preparation for an attack on Brampton Bryan, and it was probably a detachment of Woodhouse's men who appeared in front of the castle within a day or so of its capture. As Samuel More explained:

> We [were] not able to hinder them because the work did not flank being an old wall made ruined [probably an incomplete section of the curtain wall] – and burnt the lodging where Richard Steward lay, they brought ladders to scale the walls, but upon our killing of three, of which one in the place [i.e. one of the dead was left behind], they retreated and went out of the town [Hopton village], but kept courts of guard near us with horse and foot.[7]

At this time there were only 16 men in the castle, including More and Major Phillips, 'a young gentleman of sweet and comely person and admirable parts'[8] who had come from Brampton Bryan to advise on strengthening Hopton's defences. The Brampton Bryan garrison sent More twelve more men, but on seeing the Royalist forces in the vicinity, half of them turned back. Six did join More, then a further eight, making, according to his rather uncertain arithmetic, 31 men in all!

A week later Woodhouse and his men re-appeared in strength, coming into view two hours before dawn and, according to More, setting fire to the remains of Richard Steward's house. The location of the house is unknown, except that it was evidently one of the buildings close to the wall of the inner courtyard, for the Royalists apparently entered the ruins and made a breach in the courtyard wall near the base of the house's chimney. More's sentries alerted the rest of the garrison, who stood to arms and

> There we fought with the enemy at push of pike, throwing stones and shooting. They, as after some of theirs reported, being two hundred, got most of them through the breach, but not within our works, but as in a pinfold [a sheep or cattle pen], in the circumference of the burnt lodging, where we killed many, among the rest one Captain Vaughan, who as I since heard was brother-in-law to Mr Edwards of Shelton. There we repulsed them, took six muskets, ten pikes, eight clubs which they called Roundheads, boards many and six or eight ladders.[9]

Leaving behind outposts to observe the enemy, the main Royalist force withdrew to Clungunford.

Woodhouse appealed to Rupert for reinforcements. He admitted to the loss of one captain (Vaughan) and two men dead, and said that he was unable to take the castle without the aid of artillery. He may also have lost Major Henry Vaughan of his regiment. He seems to have been supplied with three pieces of artillery, probably supplied, given the interval of time involved, from Shrewsbury.

A week after the repulse of their first assault, the Royalists returned to Hopton Castle. Woodhouse had been reinforced by men from Richard Herbert's regiment, and perhaps by some of Prince Rupert's veteran 'Bluecoats'. Before the onslaught was renewed, Francis Herbert and Charles Baldwin, local Royalist gentlemen, and one of Woodhouse's officers, Captain Pindoe, were sent to speak to More and urge him to surrender. In an attempt to persuade More, Pindoe told him that he had just received a letter from the king's Secretary of State, Sir Edward Nicholas, telling him of a major defeat suffered by Parliament's Scottish allies. 'I told him', More later recounted 'I knew Secretary Nicholas well, which as he afterwards said, was the saving of my life.' More remained adamant, and next day the Royalists began emplacing their three guns.

On Monday 11 March, at 8am, a Royalist drummer approached with a summons, warning the defenders that if they 'did not yield before the shooting of one piece of ordnance' they 'could expect no quarter'. Rejecting the summons, More informed the messenger that 'we were trusted to keep it for the service of King and Parliament, by the consent of the owner, Mr Wallop, and would do it with loyalty and fidelity'.

The Royalist guns, a culverin and demi-culverin, now opened fire, in a bombardment lasting from nine in the morning until five in the afternoon. A total of 96 shots were fired, creating a breach in the courtyard wall of the castle which the garrison worked frantically to block with boughs of trees and earth.

> About five of the clock they approached the breach, which we defended, and for the space of two hours at least we fought at push of pike, musket and clubs, so that we gave them a repulse with the loss of one man, who was killed with a cannon shot, and three or four hurt. But they lost, as they afterwards confessed, in all one hundred and fifty of theirs, some said two hundred. I could not imagine we killed so many, but as they said themselves, yet we saw many fall.[10]

Next day the Royalists were given leave to remove their fallen, and both sides attempted to improve their positions for renewed action. Woodhouse's men burnt a tower which protected the water defences of the castle, possibly allowing them to drain any moat which existed. For their part, the Parliamentarians burnt 'Gregory's house', another outlying building, in order to deny its cover to the attackers.

Parliamentarian captain Priamus Davies related: 'Two great guns were sent against it [Hopton Castle] which played with great fury, but still resistance was made. Several proposals offered but all refused and Sir Michael Woodhouse, enraged, swore their ruin as Major [Williams] of the Prince's foot assured me.'[11]

Presumably several breaches had now been made in the curtain wall, for the garrison were forced back into the Great Tower, whose door they attempted to barricade. The Royalists opened fire on the working party with at least one gun, killing one man and injuring two:

> We made up the door, but they brought brown faggots to fire the porch; we threw water to quench it, but for all we could do the porch burnt, and the door began to fire, which we did not perfectly know till we came out. Our men, weary with working all night, and not out of their clothes for a fortnight's time, and the enemy gotten under us through a house of office on the south side, it was moved we should desire a parley.

The garrison asked that they be allowed to march out with arms and ammunition, but received the reply that 'we should have no conditions but to yield to the Colonel's mercy'.[12] In view of what happened next, it is important to clarify what was meant by surrendering 'to' or 'at mercy'. The 'laws of war' were ill-defined and without clear legal standing, but in general the term meant that those surrendering did so with the knowledge that their fate was entirely up to their captor. They might be released, they might be imprisoned, or they might be killed. More undoubtedly hoped that he and his men would be spared, but he may not have realised that this might not be the outcome.

Samuel More with Major Phillips and a few others went to consult in the downstairs room of the tower, moving out a good deal of lumber and supplies in order to get in. Here they could plainly hear the sound of excavating underneath, as the Royalists prepared a mine. More would later learn that this would have been exploded within two hours. This development was decisive:

> We agreed to propose to the enemy we would yield the castle upon quarter for our lives. Answer was brought that no other conditions would be yielded but to be referred to Colonel Woodhouse's mercy. We then consulted again and being brought into that condition it was thought better to yield upon those terms, than be blown up, but indeed we all thought we should only be made prisoners and did not think that such a death as hereafter shall appear was upon so many honest souls. So we told them we would yield to their mercy, only we desired safe conduct from the violence of soldiers to the Commander in Chief.[13]
>
> So we came out, and stood in order, I was committed to Lieutenant Aldersley [Woodhouse's regiment] and Major Phillips to Ensign Phillips, [Woodhouse's regiment, probably a Ludlow man] so whilst the soldiers and Henry Gregory and the rest had their arms tied, we all stayed, and then we were bidden march, so I went, and thought the rest had followed till I went over the water by Richard Steward's house towards Mr Sutton's house and then I looked back and saw none follow. I marvelled, but my thoughts were, the rest were to be examined apart; but as it seems by the relation afterwards they were stayed behind. But I was brought before Sir Michael Woodhouse, who asked me the number of the men, which I told him, and what arms and ammunition? I told him about twenty-two muskets, carabines and fowling pieces and three pistols. He asked what I thought they fought for? I told him I thought he as many other men was misled, so he commanded me to the custody of Lieutenant Aldersley, to one Glasbrook's house in the upper end of the town, where after I had been about an hour, an officer, whose name I never heard, asked me what money I knew of there hid. I told him none. He urged me and said Mr Phillips had confessed some. I told him I did know of none nor knew that Mr Phillips knew of any. So he went after some threatenings.
>
> Another came and asked me whether I desired to live? I answered it was natural to desire to live, yet I prized not my life before a good conscience. Then a little after, about three hours after the delivery of the Castle, Lieutenant Aldersley asked me how many of the soldiers I thought were sent to Shrewsbury? I told him I knew not, I conceived all were in one condition; he told me none, which I wondering at apprehended they were delivered and was somewhat cheerful. But then he answered with an oath that they were all killed, whereat I was troubled in myself, though I did not much express my sorrow, only said I hoped they were happy, or to that effect. So night growing on, I was called to eat with Lieutenant Aldersley, who indeed used me civilly. I could eat but little; then he let me lie

upon his own bed, where I lay till day break, and then I rose, and so they fell to prepare for Ludlow, whither I was brought.[14]

The killing of More's men caused a wave of outrage. Although only Parliamentarian versions of what happened survive, they make grim reading:

> Command was given that they should be bound two and three, then they were stripped naked as ever they were born, it being about the beginning of March, very cold and many of them sore wounded in defending their own works, thus they remained about an hour until the word was given that they should be left to the mercy of the common soldiers, who presently fell upon them, wounding them grievously, and drove them into a cellar unfinished, wherein was stinking water, the house being on fire over them, where they were every man of them presently massacred.[15]

William Gregory, aged over 80, 'being weak and not able to stand, they were so compassionate as to put him in a chair to cut his throat'. It was claimed on uncertain grounds that one of the prisoners managed to hide in the cellar and later escape, whilst two women who were present were allowed to go free, one of them to carry the news to Brampton Bryan. One of the women who had injured her back jumping from a window was said still be alive, 'distracted', in Ludlow in 1695.

A Parliamentarian news pamphlet, *Mercurius Britannicus*, gave further lurid details:

> Mr More was seized upon, and carried away prisoner, and the 24 [*sic*] soldiers tied back to back, and then some of them had their hands cut off, some with a hand, part of an arm, and the rest cut and mangled both on hands and arms, and then all of them thrown into a muddy pit, where as often as any of them endeavoured to raise themselves out of the mud, striving to prolong their miserable lives, they were straight by these bloody villains beat back down into the mud again with great stones, which they hurled at them, and in this sad manner lamentably perished. Two maids were in the Castle, one they killed, and the other they wounded, and let her go, bidding her to go to Brampton Castle, and tell her brother roundheads there, so they would serve them next.[16]

The Royalists tacitly admitted that the massacre had taken place, with their newsletter *Mercurius Aulicus* stating somewhat disingenuously 'Master Moore will tell you neither woman, nor child received the least hurt'.[17]

The exact reasons for the killings remained unclear. More would be told later that Woodhouse was acting on orders 'from Oxford'.[18] As we shall see it may well be that he had received instructions to make an example of the Hopton defenders, but it is much more likely that his orders came from Prince Rupert at Shrewsbury than from the king in Oxford.

Woodhouse's own attitude is rather more ambivalent. He appears to have been a convinced Royalist, at least for so long as it served his interests to be so. His regimental chaplain, Edward Symmons, was noted in his writings for taking a hard-line attitude towards the king's opponents, telling the Royalist soldiers 'your imployment is to inflict sharp punishment upon rebellious men', to be 'inexorable, and not abate one jot of the punishment commanded to inflict'. His dedication of his book to Sir Michael Woodhouse suggests that his commander shared

Symmons' views.[19] However, the fact that Sir Michael and his officers absented themselves from the actual scene of the killings and the delay of an hour before they were carried out, suggests some disquiet. There would later be reports that the rank and file of Woodhouse's men had been enraged by the heavy casualties they had suffered, amid claims that the Parliamentarians had used poisoned bullets. In such circumstances, discipline can easily break down and atrocities occur. The fact that Woodhouse's men were mainly Welsh, rather than local men, probably increased the chance of a massacre occurring.

Back in Ludlow the bells of St Laurence's were rung to celebrate the capture of Hopton Castle.[20] Some of the Royalist dead and wounded were conveyed to the town and a list of soldiers buried there clearly includes many of Woodhouse's men. Woodhouse's Lieutenant-Colonel, Richard Thurland, had been buried on 3 February, possibly a victim of disease rather than a battle casualty. The following, all called 'soldier' in the register and likely to have died from their wounds after being brought to Ludlow, were probably casualties from Hopton Castle, mainly from Woodhouse's regiment but possibly also some from Herbert's: Robert Hayter and Evan Owens (buried on 3 March); Humphrey Lloyd (10 March); John Buckly (12 March); John Lawrence, John Hoskies, William Palmer and Frauncis Davies (13 March); William Jones (18 March); Owen Jones (19 March); John Martin (20 March); Thomas Evans (23 March); Thomas Powel (25 March); Hugh Melamie (26 March); Edward Evans (28 March); Walter Fowler, captain (30 March); and Richard Davies (31 March).[21]

With Hopton Castle reduced, Brampton Bryan was the next Royalist target. According to the Parliamentarians, Woodhouse marched on it immediately after the fall of Hopton:

> this bloody regiment came vapouring, so near that some of them were slain, some unhorsed, so they wheeled about, and marched away, with their ordnance, to Shrewsbury.[22]

Dr Wright's garrison at Brampton Bryan still numbered around 50 men, together with several refugees and their dependants, and he had the additional responsibility of three Harley children within its walls. It wasn't long before Woodhouse was back, according to Captain Priamus Davies:

> This bloody butcher Woodhouse with a great army came and sat down before us; demanded our castle by summons, which our Governor refused to read or treat with such a tyrant.[23]

A second summons was also rejected, and the siege proper began during the second week of Lent. The Royalists proceeded methodically against Brampton Bryan. Troops were brought in from across the region, including the small Herefordshire regiment of Sir William Croft, Richard Herbert's men from Ludlow, possibly a detachment of Prince Rupert's regiment of Bluecoat foot, and guns from Shrewsbury under the direction of the prince's military engineer, the Walloon Bernard de Gomme. Even so, morale among the Royalists was low, as Richard Herbert explained in a letter to Prince Rupert on 17 March:

> I received orders even now, from Sir Michael Woodhouse, for my Regiment to march for Brampton Castle, which shall be obeyed, yet, the difficulty my officers had to make them march unto Hopton (for want of those necessary accommodations this bearer will

represent unto your Highness) makes me apprehend a greater difficulty now. The officers of the regiment being all of them, extremely necessitous for the pay I received by your Highness's command in Salop [Shrewsbury] 50 pounds reaching little further than to pay Sergeants, Drums, Corporals and Common Soldiers, are now worse provided to march them than they were. The consideration hereof makes humbly to beseech your Highness, to give order, the Regiment may be paid, officers and soldiers, according to the late muster, and present establishment, and this I doubt not, may preserve those I have together, until order taken to recruit the regiment. In the last place I take the boldness, to remind your Highness, of my commission for Governor of Montgomery Castle, the which I humbly desire your Highness to order may be sent unto me, by this bearer.[24]

As Herbert's letter was addressed from Montgomery, it is unclear whether Woodhouse had by now replaced Herbert as Governor of Ludlow, but gives the impression that relations between the two men were not good.

As the siege of Brampton Bryan began, the defenders burnt the church and some neighbouring houses to deny their shelter to the besiegers. The Royalists were forced to set up their quarters about a mile off, leaving 300 men from Croft's regiment to guard their siege works.

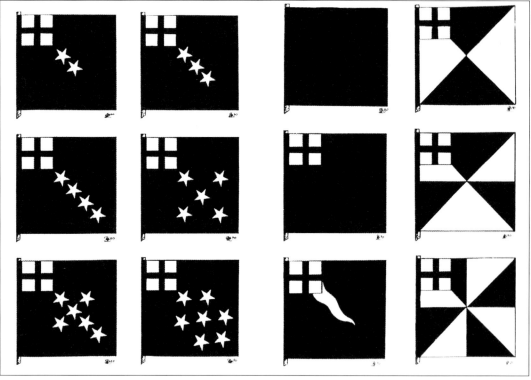

Flags or colours carried by infantry usually followed one of several recognised 'systems' of symbols differentiating between the different companies of a regiment. The flags above are from three regiments: those in the two columns on the left from one regiment, and each of the two right-hand columns from different regiments. A regiment was sometimes known by the background, or 'field' colour of its flag, e.g. 'the green regiment'.

Thirty men of the garrison then made a sortie, claiming to have killed 16 men without loss to themselves. The Royalists responded by strengthening their guard, building huts and raising gun batteries. The Parliamentarians replied with a second sally, this time by daylight, which drove the Royalists out of their trenches, and burnt their huts, killing 26 Royalists, capturing a number of muskets and returning without loss.

Woodhouse, according to the Parliamentarians 'enraged at this, posts away to Prince Rupert at Shrewsbury, tells him a great story …'.[25] Certainly Sir Michael expressed his annoyance by letter to the prince on 6 April penned 'at 9 at night'.

> May it please your Highness
> This day between one and two of the clock the rogues made a sally out of the Castle. Colonel Croft his men had the approaches, both officer and soldier run, quitted the works. Some pioneers were killed; not above two soldiers killed for they were swift of foot and left twenty muskets, the rogues were in our court of guards betimes to throw down our works, fired our battery, but before they could accomplish anything to purpose of their desires, I was with them and regained the works again, and shall this night make all up again with my own men, for pioneers to purpose I cannot get. If your Highness intends to have this Castle, you must be pleased to send me men, which will defend what we make, and fight, those men which are ordered for me I am confident will serve me still at this rate, all the officers are in fault of theirs, wherefore I desire to know of your Highness where they shall be hanged.
>
> I have taken a woman that was sent out of the Castle with a letter to a man of this County for relief from Gloucester, the man I have likewise. He denies any letter to be returned by him from her, and she justifies the delivery of it to her hand, the quean was returning in man's apparel and offered [pretended] to be a soldier in Croft his company. I desire your Highness's pleasure concerning them. Those of my men are now upon the place and shall not stir, to have another battery burnt this was the second, and I hope your Highness will not let the poor remainder I have be tired out, or the Castle left for want of good men, when they are to be had, if a greater concern commands them not in another way.
>
> When there is anything good your Highness shall have it sooner. Monsieur De Gomme is of my opinion that in 8 days the Castle may be in our hands if we had wherewithal.[26]

The Parliamentarians claimed two more successful sallies before Woodhouse was reinforced 'with the Red Green and Blue Regiments, and great ordnance which he speedily planted, and a multitude of pioneers and colliers that began to mine'.[27]

The increased numbers of besiegers made it impossible for the garrison to mount any more sorties, and the Royalist guns were able to begin their bombardment without interruption. On the first day they fired 87 shot, some of 20lb or 24lb weight.

> These made our walls begin to reel, which we lined with earth. The next day they continued shooting as fast as they could discharge, until with a musket bullet through the port hole we shot their cannonier. Five days together they followed the breach, which was very great and fair to enter, but their hearts failed them.[28]

The defenders had been promised relief from Gloucester within three days, and held on grimly. The Royalists under cover of darkness had set fire to the timber barricades which the defenders had filled the breach with, and opened fire on the Parliamentarians as they struggled to extinguish the flames, but caused no losses. Concerned about reports that a Parliamentarian relief force was approaching Hereford, Sir Michael Woodhouse explained to Prince Rupert, in a letter written early on the morning of 12 April:

> I … do think it fit to declare to your highness, that if they advance without I receive assistance to the purpose I cannot make good the place I am engaged in, the last night about 12 of the clock I attempted to fire the breach it being filled with timber, and did it, but the rogues put it again with much ado. I had a sergeant shot, and yesterday one Canoneer, the last night the miners lodged themselves, and if I be left alone, doubt not of the place.[29]

Rupert evidently responded favourably, for at 1pm on 14 April, Woodhouse wrote to him:

> This day at twelve of the clock I received your Letter, and give your Highness humble thanks for sending more men, for we were tired out, the last night we were with our mine under the graf, and find several springs that hinder much, but notwithstanding I hope towards the latter end of this week to have the mine sprung …[30]

Within the next couple of days Sir William Vavasour, Colonel General and effective commander under Lord Herbert of Royalist forces in south Wales and the southern Marches, arrived at Brampton. Vavasour had commanded a regiment in the Scots War of 1640, suggesting some previous military experience, and joined the king in 1642. He had been captured at the Battle of Edgehill but escaped in April 1643, and in June was sent to assist Lord Herbert.

Meanwhile the defenders of Brampton Bryan still held out, despite the non-appearance of the hoped-for relief – 'we yet resolved to defend the breach to the very last man, for their cruelty at Hopton Castle encouraged us to die like men rather than to rely on their mercies'. For another three days the garrison held the breach, with constant alarms both day and night,

> … so that we were all tired from want of sleep. Twice on one night, their whole army, which was very great, cried 'Fall on!', 'Fall on !' so loud as if hell itself were broke loose, discharging such volleys of shot that no rest could be had. When the alarm was ended, we laughed so heartily in the breach hollering that barking dogs seldom bite, that we heard them damn themselves but the devil was in us. [The Royalists now began to] terrify us [with their mines] swearing most horribly that they would blow us up to the devil; we replied that the devil was below, and bid them come like men and enter their breach or be silent, for fain we would have slept …[31]

The Royalists in fact seem to have had little appetite to assault the breach, and instead decided to ask Samuel More, still a prisoner in Ludlow Castle, to intervene. As More related:

> Captain Dean, in Sir Michael Woodhouse's regiment, pretended to come to see me, and in discourse told me they had battered the castle, so as they were ready to enter and were ready to spring a mine, and if I desired to have them saved, I might do well to persuade

them to yield. I told him I had no means to write; he said he would convey the letter. I told him then I would write what I heard. So I told Dr Wright that I heard Brampton Castle was not like to hold out long, and that conditions were granted, better sought timely than stay too long, but I left it to his more wise consideration. He answered me that he heard Sir Michael Woodhouse break his conditions with me, for he promised quarter as he heard, and therefore he would not treat with him. I replied that we were referred to his mercy; so then they treated and agreed. I hope it saved blood, but I confess I had much reluctance with myself, knowing it was their own ends they sought, and therefore I wrote warily, expressing I was close prisoner.[32]

Wright was somewhat wary as well, even though More had confirmed that the conditions offered at Hopton had not been given 'under hand and seal'. However terms were agreed under which the lives of all at Brampton Bryan would be spared, although they would be taken prisoner.

But the defenders were still in danger. Two hours after terms were agreed, a message arrived from Prince Rupert instructing that all the men in the castle should be hanged. The Royalist commanders called a council of war, at which it appears some felt that Rupert's orders had to be obeyed. Given his previous record, it is very likely that Woodhouse was among those arguing in favour of this course of action. But it appears that the Herefordshire Royalist leaders were unhappy about killing their neighbours in cold blood, and Sir William Vavasour decided that as terms had already been agreed, then they must be honoured. Clearly intending to pacify the prince, Vavasour wrote to him: 'I hope he [Wright] may redeem a gallant man [by a prisoner exchange] however, the law may hang him …'. Two days later, in further justification, he wrote:

> Sir,
> The rebels at Brampton had discovered the candle in the mine, so that I hope your Highness is not offended that they were treated withal, for certainly they might have made it a tedious work: I did not pretend to anything in the Castle. Sir Michael Woodhouse hath all the prisoners …[33]

News of the capture of Brampton Bryan resulted in another celebratory peal of bells at St Laurence's in Ludlow. Soon afterwards the captured garrison were marched into the town 'where the inhabitants baited us like bears, and demanded where our God was'.[34] The prisoners taken included Lieutenant-Colonel Nathaniel Wright, Captains John Hakluit, Henry Archibold and Priamus Davies, Thomas Harley (son of Sir Robert), his sisters Dorothy and Margaret, and Monsieur Peter Vachan (possibly a French Huguenot tutor to Thomas Harley), and nearly one hundred others (presumably including relations of members of the garrison, and possibly others who had come in after the surrender of Hopton Castle).[35] They were soon afterwards moved on to imprisonment in Shrewsbury and Chester.

As Vavasour's letter above indicated, Woodhouse had already written to Rupert on 17 April just after terms were agreed and the prince's orders arrived:

> This day Sir William Vavasour came to my quarters and advised me to send to the Castle once more which I did with him, and it wrought with them for the delivery of the place

giving them their lives and to be at your Highness's pleasure, we were treating with them before your highness's letter came to my hands which I am sorry for, but your command shall be obeyed for the ward and children, for Wright he may get an honest man Sir Richard Willys enlarged. I cannot give your highness a particular account of what is here, but by appearance little, Sir I desire your orders concerning the men from Oswestry, Herbert's or Russell's, for those your Highness sent me they shall return tomorrow towards Salop [Shrewsbury], and for the Cannon that your Highness will give me order for them likewise ...

I desire your highness's commands whether or not you will have a garrison kept here and likewise in Hopton Castle, this place is strong and I believe cause[s] these parts to bring in their contributions, and a good company may be had here by your Highness's order in a short time.[36]

As to whether to garrison Brampton Bryan and Hopton Castles, Rupert was actually in the process of reducing the number of garrisons in the Marches so as to muster an army for his planned summer campaign. He intended to reconquer Lancashire and assist the Marquis of Newcastle who was struggling to contain the Scottish invasion of north-east England, at the same time countering the resurgent Yorkshire Parliamentarians under the Fairfaxes. Orders were therefore given that both castles should be 'slighted'.

The Parliamentarians claimed that the capture of Brampton Bryan cost the Royalists 400 men. This seems likely to have been a considerable exaggeration, but the burial register of St Laurence's once again includes soldiers who most probably died of their wounds in the town after being conveyed from the siege, including John Saunders (16 April), Thomas Lewis (22 April), Robert Hatter (3 May), Griffith Davies (6 May), Owen Jones and Edward Tomkins (12 May).[37] It was a significantly shorter list than that which had followed the siege of Hopton Castle.

Prince Rupert visited Ludlow on Easter Monday (22 April 1644), his arrival celebrated by the ringing of the church bells.[38] There was no doubt an inquest into what had happened at Brampton Bryan, but the visit was also part of Rupert's wider re-organisation of the command structure in Wales and the Marches before he commenced his campaign in the north of England. Professional soldiers were appointed as governors of several key garrisons. Sir Lewis Kirke took command at Bridgnorth; a colonel from the English army in Ireland, Sir Fulke Hunckes became Governor of Shrewsbury in place of Sir Francis Ottley; Sir Abraham Shipman, former Governor of Chester, took over at Oswestry; and Rupert's right-hand man, Will Legge at Chester. Richard Herbert was removed as Governor of Ludlow, though, in a decision he was shortly to have cause to regret, Rupert did not accede to his request to be governor of Montgomery Castle, allowing Richard's father, the eccentric and scholarly Lord Herbert, to remain in possession. Richard was instead made Governor of Aberystwyth Castle, a sideways move rather than a promotion. Sir Michael Woodhouse was appointed as Governor of Ludlow, probably with effect from 28 April. He would prove an effective, if uncompromising, Governor, but initially he was busy with the aftermath of the capture of Hopton and Brampton Bryan Castles, acting with perhaps surprising moderation for a man with such a 'bloody' reputation.

Samuel More, though soon to be exchanged, was still a prisoner, probably in the Constable's house (now Castle Lodge) in Ludlow, but:

Castle Lodge, Ludlow. Residence of the 'porter', or 'constable' of Ludlow Castle, the Lodge was evidently also used during the Civil War to house prominent Parliamentarian prisoners, among them Samuel More, Governor of Hopton Castle.

After Brampton Castle was taken I had my liberty to speak more freely and to come into the kitchen and speak with the people of the house, and so continued a while until my exchange; only Mr [Edward] Symmonds, a minister of Essex that was Sir Michael Wood-house's chaplain, came to see me and got me so much liberty as to go to the chapel in the castle two Sabbath days, otherwise I was not permitted to go out of the lodge. I moved Mr Symmonds that since my estate was sequestered and my house plundered I might be allowed [money] out of my estate to pay for my diet. This was also granted, after that time which was about a fortnight and three days before my release, but the rest of the time I paid.[39]

Sir Robert Harley's three younger children, Thomas, Margaret and Dorothy, were lodged in the castle. Neither Woodhouse nor Prince Rupert evidently had any wish to keep them longer than necessary, but arrangements for their release took some time, the Herefordshire Royalist Sir John Scudamore, a pre-war neighbour and acquaintance of the Harleys, acting as go-between. The children were being cared for by an Elizabeth Bletchley, evidently a member of the Brampton Bryan household, perhaps the girls' governess, for Sir John wrote to her, at Ludlow Castle, in May:

I have received yours and Sir Michael Woodhouse's letters and am very glad yours and my sweet cousins' freedom is so near. I think it fit that you get Sir Michael Woodhouse to give a pass to a messenger to be presently sent away to Sir Robert Harley to procure the Earl of Essex's pass for all [of] you, and for such a friend as you shall make choice of and prevail with to bring you up. As also to send to Sir Robert to send a hackney coach for you. God willing, I shall not fail to wait upon you on Tuesday next. My service, I pray, to my sweet cousins.[40]

On 30 May Thomas Harley wrote to Colonel Edward Massey, Parliamentarian Governor of Gloucester:

Ludlow Castle. – I and my two sisters, with those that are with us, since Brampton Castle was taken having been at Ludlow Castle, where we have been nobly used by Sir Michael Woodhouse, the governor, are now set at liberty by him to pass to London. Therefore I desire that if you cannot send a coach to Hereford for us, that you will give a safe pass for a coach and horses which shall bring us thither, and Sir John Scudamore, who is pleased to do the favour for our safer conduct, to come with us, and for his servants and horses' safe return.[41]

Sir John Scudamore (1st Viscount Scudamore, 1601-71). A relative of the Harley family, and rather half-hearted Royalist leader in Herefordshire, Scudamore had acted as an intermediary between Lady Harley and the besiegers in 1643.

By now Samuel More had been exchanged, and, also in May, wrote to Thomas:

I sent you a note from Stafford that my Lord Brereton's [a leading Cheshire Royalist] son is freed from his imprisonment by my Lord Denbigh [Parliamentarian general in the Midlands], whose enlargement I do conceive will begat yours and your sweet sisters. I hope also your servants, Samuel Shilton and William Bagley, shall have leave to wait on you to your father.

I was not free from my imprisonment till Saturday sevennight, and I sent to you from Stafford, whither I was brought, but lest that should not come to you I send this to kiss your hand.[42]

There were however delays in arranging the children's journey to London, and on 7 June, still in Ludlow Castle, Thomas Harley wrote to Sir John Scudamore at Hereford:

Our not hearing from you since Monday is the reason why we send this messenger to you, by whom we desire to hear if yet you have heard anything from Gloucester in answer to our letters thither; and when you do we shall be very glad to see you there.[43]

There were further problems, partly, as we shall see, because fighting had flared up in the vicinity of Gloucester. On 10 June Lady Scudamore explained to Thomas:

Sweet Cousin, I have received your letter directed unto my husband; upon Friday last he went towards Worcester, but is not yet returned; all that I can say concerning your business is this: our Governor here, Colonel [Nicholas] Minn, went unto Monmouth about nine days past, with purpose to send a trumpeter to Gloucester with all the letters, which he did, and since is returned hither to Hereford, but can hear nothing of the messenger since he went. Whereupon I told my husband that perhaps the trumpeter might be detained till the Governor of Gloucester returns from Malmesbury; but he saith that the Governor came back upon Tuesday last. This is all I can say. It may be you see my husband before I shall, for I hoped he would have returned yesterday. I desire you to remember my service to your little sweet sisters and the gentlewoman with them.[44]

However, a week later matters were progressing, and on 18 June Sir Michael Woodhouse wrote from Ludlow Castle to Sir John Scudamore:

In pursuance of an order given unto me by his Highness the Prince Rupert to set at liberty the bodies of Thomas Harley, gentleman, Dorothy and Margaret his sisters – the children of Sir Robert Harley, knight of the Bath – who were amongst others taken prisoners in Brampton Bryan Castle, in the county of Hereford, by his Majesty's forces under my command, it is therefore by me ordered and I desire and require you being their near kinsman, to take into your charge and custody the bodies of the aforementioned persons, and to take such course as you shall think fit for the conveyance of them to their said father in London, or elsewhere.[45]

Two days later Thomas Harley informed Colonel Edward Massey at Gloucester, writing from the Scudamore home at Holme Lacy:

I received your letter and give you many thanks for your expression of love and kindness to us. We are come from Ludlow Castle, and intend, God willing, to go to London. Therefore I desire you, Sir, you will do us the favour to send to my Lord of Essex – who I hear is not far from Gloucester – for one pass for my sisters, myself and our company to London, and another pass for Sir John Scudamore – who doth not only accommodate us for our journey, but himself doth us that favour to come with us – and his two servants to go up to London, and for the return of him, his servants, coach and horses.[46]

On 30 June Thomas, now at Northampton, was able at last to tell his father:

I must humbly beg pardon that I have not presented my humble duty to you and acquainted you how it was with us. I thank God my sisters and I are very well, and though God hath afflicted us – which I pray God to sanctify us – yet He hath been very merciful to us, so that among our enemies we received favour; and it is no small mercy to us that God continues health to you and you to us. Sir, after we had been at Ludlow Castle eight weeks and more, we were released to go to London, and Sir John Scudamore to take care to convey us thither – who hath shown us much kindness, and hath lent his coach and horses to bring us, and himself comes with us.

We came out of Ludlow on Tuesday 18 June, and came to Holm[e] Lacy, where we were used exceedingly kindly by my Lady Scudamore, and tarried there till the Saturday following; and from thence went to Gloucester, where we tarried till Thursday after, and then went to Sudeley Castle, on Friday to Warwick, and on Saturday we came safe to Northampton, where we are now; and I hope God will bring us safe to you, to our great joy and comfort after so many afflictions. Sir, my brother Robert is very well and presents his humble duty to you. We met with him at Gloucester, where not being well he tarried there, and because he could not pass safe to the army he came with us as far as Warwick.[47]

Clearly if the Harley children, and also apparently officer prisoners, were well-treated, the same conditions were not necessarily applied to other captives in Ludlow during the war. Captain Wingate, one officer held there, recounted:

Some other Prisoners they have also put in a close Prison [possibly the dungeon under one of the towers of Broad Gate], using them in the extremist cruelty that may be devised, allowing them only bread and water for their sustestation, and so little that if they long continue there, they will be starved to death.[48]

6   Ludlow at War

As well dealing with the matter of the Harley children, Sir Michael Woodhouse will have been settling into his new role as Governor of Ludlow.

The role of a town's governor in the English Civil War deserves some explanation, especially as the exact extent of his powers and responsibilities was not always entirely clear even to contemporaries. All military units in a garrison, and its fortifications, including at Ludlow the crown-owned castle, came under the governor's control, along with all defence measures. In the early stages of the war, as evidently happened at Ludlow in the case of Thomas Fisher and at Shrewsbury with Francis Ottley, the governor might be appointed by the civil authorities of a town, and so be responsible to them. This led increasingly to problems, with a governor finding himself caught between the often conflicting demands of king (or Parliament) and the authorities in his town. One of Prince Rupert's first actions on assuming command on the Welsh Border was, as we have seen, for the most part to replace these appointees with professional soldiers who were answerable primarily to the crown, via the prince as Lord President of Wales and the Marches.

A governor was also responsible for civilian matters within his garrison, at least so far as they impacted on military concerns. As far as possible, because it was much more difficult to operate in opposition to them, a wise governor would try to work in consultation with the civic authorities in his town, whilst retaining sole control of any castle there.

However, such co-operation often became fraught when a garrison was under acute military threat. In such situations, defence needs were often in conflict with civilian interests. For example, the governor might require the dismantling or destruction of individual houses and other buildings, and often entire suburbs, to deny their cover to the enemy. Understandably civilians in some cases might try to hinder such actions. In the case of a siege, the rationing of food supplies could also lead to growing discontent. In 1646 Lord Byron at Chester and Henry Washington at Worcester would encounter disaffection culminating in actual riot in such circumstances.

A good deal often depended upon the personality of the individual governor. The professional soldiers such as Sir Michael Woodhouse appointed by Prince Rupert were not noted for tact and diplomacy when dealing with civilians. On the whole, however, Woodhouse had fewer problems with the council in Ludlow than were encountered by some of his counterparts elsewhere. The Ludlow corporation appears usually to have been fairly subservient, if not always enthusiastic. As we shall see there were periodic complaints over that perennial cause of discontent, the billeting of soldiers on householders as well as various other issues, but there

Ludlow Castle: the North range of buildings, including the Tudor Lodgings.
These had been reconstructed in the 16th century to house senior officials of the Council in the
Marches, and during the Civil War provided accommodation for the governors of Ludlow
and visiting dignitaries including King Charles and Prince Rupert.

does not appear ever to have been open rebellion in Ludlow as happened in other towns. The surrounding countryside was a different matter. It does seem though that problems here were sparked more by the actions of officers not under Woodhouse's direct control.

Woodhouse was apparently somewhat less rapacious than some of his colleagues and at least made some attempt to act under the rule of law. Both he and the people of Ludlow were also fortunate in not having to face the kind of prolonged siege that occurred elsewhere.

As the king's representative in Ludlow, Woodhouse would have resided in the castle rather than in what is now Castle Lodge outside its walls. There is no reference to Sir Michael being married, so he very possibly occupied either one of the suites of rooms in the Tudor Lodgings, or possibly the Judges' Lodgings. It is likely that the rooms intended for the Lord President of the Council in the Marches were used to accommodate Prince Rupert and King Charles on their visits to the town.[1]

Work on repairing Ludlow's defences had already begun during the spring and summer of 1643. As well as the earth defences which the townspeople had been ordered to construct, the bailiffs' accounts also list repairs to the walls and gates, with loopholes made in the latter for muskets, and 'coals, fires and candles' bought for soldiers and townsmen mounting guard at night. Repairs to the defences would have been an ongoing expense, and Woodhouse may at this time have ordered the dismantling of several houses in Castle Square, one the home of a Parliamentarian sympathiser, in order to improve the line of fire from the castle, where guns from Bringewood and Bouldon Forges were evidently mounted.[2]

The role of the townsmen in the garrison of Ludlow is not entirely clear. In some garrisons, such as Chester, the male population was in theory exempt from impressment into the Royalist field armies on condition that they served in 'town regiments', supposed, again often more in theory than in practice, to be required only to serve in their own locality. There is no record of such an arrangement at Ludlow, but, in 1646, a Parliamentarian account refers to 500 townsmen among Ludlow's defenders, which would approximate to the entire male population between the ages of 16 and 60.

Orders were certainly given on more than one occasion for men to be 'pressed' from the town, and a number of Ludlow residents later compounded – paying fines – after the war for 'delinquency' – that is for supporting the Royalist cause, in their cases by serving in Royalist forces away from Ludlow. At least thirteen were tradesmen, seven of whom, including William Colbach of Broad Street who was in the Stokesay Castle garrison in 1645, were engaged in the leather trade. Roger and Thomas Powis, sons of Alderman Edward Powis, another tanner, served with the Royalist forces at the capture of Brampton Bryan.[3] Thomas Fisher, as we have seen, raised a company for the defence of the town, probably formed around men of the Trained Band, and later, evidently on Prince Rupert's orders, the town was instructed to raise a company of twenty-two men, six of them furnished with horses, arms and equipment, under Charles Baldwyn. Given that both Richard Herbert's and Sir Michael Woodhouse's regiments were under-strength, it was inevitable that Ludlow men should find themselves enlisted in the ranks of both.[4]

The permanent presence of firstly Richard Herbert's 'regular' troops, followed by those of Woodhouse, the frequent initially short-term quartering of other units and the jurisdiction of military governors resulted in increasing inconvenience and some hardship for the townspeople. At the end of 1643, Mary Colbach, widow of a former alderman, complained that 'there hath been a turf dugged out [from her meadow in Broad Linney] and taken away to the work of the castle by Sir Michael Woodhouse'. Probably it was used to line the inner side of a section of the walls as a defence against artillery fire. Six months later, John Walker, a carpenter living in Castle Ward, testified that he had been 'damnified by the quartering of Colonel Woodhouse his soldiers and the taking away of my pales [timber] to the value of £13 10s'.[5]

The townspeople also found themselves caught up in both Prince Rupert's preparations for his campaign in the north and the opening weeks of the king's 1644 campaign in the Midlands. An undated order to the bailiffs from the county commissioners to press men may relate to this time. They were to muster 'all men of able bodies 16-60, except clergy to appear before us with all guns weapons and arms as they have … to the intent that fifty of the ablest of body, and best equipped' be enlisted in the king's forces. An unspecified sum of money was also to be raised to be paid to John Kirk, the Town Clerk, to purchase ammunition 'for the defence of these parts of the county'.[6] The conscription of 50 of its men, even if in some cases these may have been replaced by hired substitutes or strangers and vagrants rounded up by the constables, would have been a severe blow to Ludlow. Nor was this the end of such demands, for in April came another order from Prince Rupert. The bailiffs were to muster '26 soldiers in [for] His Majesty's Army of such condition and quality as by your former instructions you were to [provide], and bring them to the Town Hall in Shrewsbury on Thursday next, being the 2nd of May, at 9 a.m, that out of them we may make choice of so many as are required by the said Commissioners'.[7] The Ludlow bailiffs were also instructed to provide horses and carts for the prince's train of artillery 'so often as you shall be given convenient notice'.[8]

The names, and fates, of most of these men are unknown, but many of them must have marched with Rupert's army in its advance on Lancashire in May and June, have been present at the 'Bolton Massacre' on 28 May, when the town was stormed by the Royalists, as well as the bitterly contested siege of Liverpool in the following month. Some would also be at the Battle of Marston Moor – but that lay a little in the future.

To the south-west of Ludlow King Charles was facing his greatest crisis of the war so far, when the combined Parliamentarian armies of the Earl of Essex and Sir William Waller closed in around Oxford, forcing the king and the bulk of his army to make a perilous night march to the greater safety of Worcester and the Severn Valley. With a Royalist army of around 7,000 men in and around Worcester, all the neighbouring Royalist-controlled areas were called for supplies. On 14 June the Ludlow bailiffs received the king's command to send with all possible speed to Worcester 'all kinds of provision of victuals' and to cause a 'good store of Biscuit to be baked and good quantity of Butter, Cheese, Bacon and Meal to be provided and sent forthwith'. The supplies were to be delivered to the Governor of Worcester, Sir Gilbert Gerard, and payment, it was promised, would be made by the High Sheriff of Worcestershire from a fund known as the 'Subsistence Money'.[9]

As the king moved on northwards up the Severn to Bewdley, there seemed a possibility of Ludlow being caught up in the anticipated fighting. On 15 June Woodhouse ordered the bailiffs to 'forthwith press sufficient labouring men and materials fitting for the making up of the town walls and those gates which are most dangerous for the approach of the Enemy'.[10]

Musketeer. This individual who c ould have served with either side. Woollen caps of the type he is wearing were probably especially common among soldiers in the Welsh Marches, as Bewdley was a noted centre for their manufacture.

In the event the crisis passed off, as the king doubled back to Oxford and on 29 June at Cropredy Bridge near Banbury in Oxfordshire inflicted a sufficiently severe mauling on Waller's army to render it ineffective for the rest of the summer.

Whilst the victory provided the Royalists with some comfort, in other respects their position in Shropshire and the Welsh Marches was deteriorating. In July Parliamentarian forces captured Oswestry, described as the 'key which opens the door into Wales', and attempts at its recovery by the Royalists at Shrewsbury, weakened by the numbers of troops drawn off by Prince Rupert for his northern campaign, were defeated with loss. Still worse was the news of the great defeat at Marston Moor on 2 July suffered by Prince Rupert. This not only saw the destruction of the Royalist Northern Army and any meaningful Royalist presence in the north of England, but it also placed the king's position in the Welsh Marches under increasing threat.

Prince Rupert returned to Chester with the remnants of his army, but meeting with little success in recruiting, headed on south to Bristol to regroup. In his absence, the Royalist position in Lancashire and Cheshire steadily worsened. In Herefordshire, Nicholas Mynne, an experienced soldier from the army in Ireland who Rupert had placed in command, was defeated and killed by forces under Edward Massey at Redmarley in Gloucestershire in August, leaving Herefordshire increasingly vulnerable to raids from Parliamentarian Gloucester.

More bad tidings came in September. Parliamentarian forces under Sir Thomas Myddleton of Chirk, theoretically commanding in north Wales, together with Shropshire troops led by Colonel Thomas Mytton, had for some time been operating in Montgomeryshire. On 5 September they summoned Lord Herbert to surrender Montgomery Castle. The eccentric scholar proved to have no taste for the perils of battle. On condition that his library was left undisturbed, he surrendered the castle and departed for his home in London.

The news was greeted with fury and consternation by the Royalists, not least by Colonel Richard Herbert, who, it will be recalled, had in the spring petitioned Prince Rupert for the post of Governor in preference to his father. The loss of Montgomery seriously hindered the Royalist line of supply from Bristol to Shrewsbury and Chester, as well as exposing much of mid Wales and central Shropshire to attack.

Lord Byron, commanding in the area in Rupert's absence, mustered troops from Chester, Shrewsbury and other garrisons in an attempt to retake Montgomery. Among them was a detachment of Woodhouse's regiment from Ludlow. It probably consisted of at least two companies under Woodhouse's Major, John Williams, including his own and that of Captain

Montgomery Castle. Lying on one of the principal Royalist supply routes between Bristol and Chester, and controlling the approaches to central Wales, the loss of the castle in September 1644 was a major blow to the king's forces.

John, Lord Byron (1600-52). Eldest of seven brothers who fought for King Charles, Byron was a notable cavalry commander. Unfairly blamed by Prince Rupert for the defeat at Marston Moor, Byron redeemed his reputation with his stubborn defence of Chester in the later stages of the war.

Gerard Dannet. Dannet came from Broseley in Shropshire, and his company probably included men from the Ludlow area.

Byron laid siege to the castle on 16 September. The following day a hastily-mustered relief force arrived, drawn from Parliamentarian troops in Cheshire, Shropshire, Lancashire and as far away as Yorkshire. Byron initially withdrew to the high ground around the old hill fort of Frith Ffaldwyn to the west of Montgomery, but on 18 September, seeing that much of the Parliamentarian horse was absent foraging, he launched an all-out attack with the aim of trapping the enemy against the River Camlad.

The details of the ensuing engagement remain obscure. It seems that the Cheshire musketeers of Sir William Brereton fired a potentially devastating volley of musket shots, which fell short, and the Royalist foot, who included large numbers of pikemen, closed with them in hand-to-hand combat. At first the advantage lay with Byron's men, and the Parliamentarians were pushed back steadily. However the tide of battle abruptly turned, for reasons which are not entirely clear.

View northwards from Montgomery Castle across the site of the battlefield.

Most probably the foraging Parliamentarian horse returned, and the Royalist cavalry, notably the regiment led by Sir William Vaughan, a veteran of the war in Ireland, who according to one Royalist account had played a principal role in bringing on the battle in the first place, broke and fled.

Left unsupported, the Royalist foot, a mixture of raw Welsh troops and the surviving veterans from Ireland, were almost all killed or captured, only around 100 escaping to Shrewsbury . Major Williams of Woodhouse's regiment was captured (though later exchanged), along with Lieutenant Aldersley and Ensigns Dannet Bishop, a relative of Captain Dannet, and Andrew Williams, of Major Williams' company. The following soldiers recorded as being buried at Ludlow may have been casualties from the engagement at Montgomery: Thomas Clarke (1 October), William Morgan (19 October), William Brace (20 October) and John Evans (24 October). Woodhouse's regiment was undoubtedly significantly reduced in numbers by its losses at Montgomery, and new recruits will have proved difficult to find.[11]

The effects of the defeat were disastrous for the Royalists in the Marches. Considered in local terms to be a worse reverse than Marston Moor, Montgomery forced the Royalists firmly on to the defensive. Henceforward they could do little more than attempt, with increasingly difficulty, to hold their ground.

Even before the defeat at Montgomery, a Royalist officer, Henry Osbourne, wrote to Rupert from Ludlow on 4 September that 'the county [is] very much allied since the enemy hath gained upon them. The Malignancy which hath late hid in many men's hearts hath now burst forth into a manifest expression.'[12]

The evidence of a downturn in Royalist fortunes also led to an increasing loss of support among the local population. We have seen how, even in the case of predominantly Royalist Ludlow, there was often reluctance to meet all of the demands made on the townspeople. Disillusionment had grown too as a result of the harsher 'military-style' regime introduced by the professional soldiers whom Rupert had appointed to key positions. Whilst they appeared in the ascendancy, Rupert's commanders were generally able to impose their will, but it was now becoming increasingly difficult. Even during the summer there had been signs of this; Kirke's men from Bridgnorth had met with violent opposition when attempting to collect taxes in nearby Shifnal, whilst both Hunckes and his successor, Sir Michael Earnley, found the Shrewsbury population hostile. On 21 October Earnley wrote to Prince Rupert: 'Since the disaster at Montgomery the edge of the gentry is much blunted; the county's loyalty is strangely abated, they begin to warp to the enemy's party.'[13]

The defeat at Montgomery certainly hastened the process. In the area north of Ludlow, particular discontent resulted from the actions of a Colonel John (or Jan) Van Gerris. In one account he is called 'Van Bynissy', which has led to some confusion, but it seems that both versions refer to the same individual. A Dutch professional soldier who had begun the war serving with the Parliamentarians but who had defected to the Royalists along with his commander at the start of the Battle of Edgehill in 1642, Van Gerris had then served briefly in Ireland. Returning to England probably early in 1644, Van Gerris was a typical example of the kind of mercenary professional soldier whom Prince Rupert favoured, with no ties to or sympathy with local civilians. The Dutchman was now commissioned as colonel of a regiment of horse, which was probably an understrength unit composed of men similar to Van Gerris himself, and sent to 'protect' the area around Bishop's Castle from incursions by the Parliamentarian forces in Powys.[14] Van Gerris proved to be uncontrollable, and his depredations on the local population caused Sir Michael Woodhouse to write, in October, a letter of protest to Prince Rupert:

> Since my last letters presented to your Highness of the loss and ill-success of Montgomery, we have no appearance of an alteration for the better, being in pursuit of our former misfortunes. Red Castle [Powis Castle] is now delivered up to the enemy without a shot. What is done with my Lord Powis we hear not yet. I must further signify unto your Highness, that if I had not been quick, my Lord Craven's Castle [Stokesay Castle] had been gone likewise, for it was made appear to me by the Gentlemen of these parts, that two days, one after another, a trumpet of the enemies' was seen in this castle, and a general assurance of the country given me that the place was suddenly to be betrayed, I sent for Mr Baker, who would observe no man's order but your Highness, and in a rebellious mutinous way appeared so I thought fit being petitioned by all the gentry of these parts, to secure the place with my own men, and put his out, which men had resolved to turn mine out the same night following.
>
> Sir, I humbly desire to know whether you approve of my action in this particular, that accordingly I may proceed.
>
> I have put a garrison within a mile of Bishop's Castle [at Lea] but I am afraid shall be forced to withdraw it again, for I can get no horse to stay with them, notwithstanding the place secure enough and to be made stronger, I was assigned Vangarie's [Van Gerris] horse but he refused to obey Sir Michael Ernley's order, or any but your Highness, he is quartered to destroy and not advance the service. I humbly beseech your Highness to take it into your consideration, and to let me have an order for his horse or some other to be with me, otherwise we must be starved, the country already refusing contribution. I humbly desire your Highness to think of sending some ammunition hither otherwise we shall be in too ill a condition to defend this place as we ought.
>
> Thus craving your Highness's pardon for this troublesome letter I humbly take leave as your Highness's most faithful and ever obedient servant.[15]

The garrison commander at Lea Hall at this time was Colonel John (or Giovanni) Devalier, a Florentine mercenary who had been a captain in Sir William Vaughan's Regiment of Horse in Ireland and had come over to England with it in February 1644. Sometime afterwards, Devalier was commissioned as a colonel by Prince Rupert and his ruthless approach, which helped spark mounting local discontent, is demonstrated by some surviving messages from Devalier to the neighbouring constables:

> These are in His Majestie's name to will and command you to bring into my Garrison of Lea Hall, on Monday next, for the week's provision being the 22nd of November, being Friday, as agreed by the Gentlemen of the County, as is mentioned in this warrant; viz:- one quarter of beef, one side of mutton, three strikes of oats, two of rye, fourteen pounds of cheese, seven pounds of butter, one couple of poultry, and in money 5s, which if you refuse you may expect my coming to fetch it, for which this shall be my warrant this 19th of November.
>
> J. Devilliers

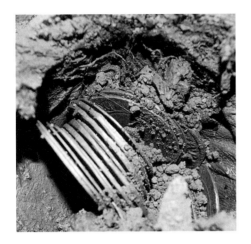

And a week later:

> To the Petty Constable of Walcott and Stockton. In regard that I was fully resolved to send unto the several towns within the whole divisions to fetch in my whole contributions both for this month and the remainder that was behind for last month, upon further consideration and the request of the High Constable and the other gentlemen of the Country, I will forbear, and give you time until Thursday next, to bring it in; otherwise I will forbear no longer, and if any mischief befall you by my soldiers in going forth, you must blame yourselves for it, and stand to the peril.[16]

Devalier was transferred to Caus Castle in December and replaced at Lea Hall by one of his officers, Captain David Lloyd, who so far as the neighbouring villagers were concerned was hardly an improvement. Supplies seem to have been sent to Lea Hall as ordered in December 1644, but in January 1645 Lloyd informed the Constable of Stockton:

> This is to certify you that I returned a warrant from the hand of the right worthy Captain Devilliers Governor of Lea Hall, whereby I am to certify you, that if you come not in between this and Monday next, to bring in your accounts, and do bring in your arrears, if not, he threatens to burn all the books, and make you pay all anew, and so I remain your loving friend, David Lloyd, Marton Hall, 23rd of January 1645.[17]

At the very least a widespread feeling of unease at the level of unrest in the Ludlow area is evidenced by the discovery by a metal detectorist in January 2011 of the 'Bitterley Hoard' near the village of that name in Corvedale. The 'hoard', buried in the remains of a leather purse in an earthenware pot, consists of one gold and 137 silver coins, dating from the reign of Edward VI through to products of the Royalist mint established at Bristol in the late summer of 1643. The hoard does not represent huge wealth, perhaps enough to buy two horses. As Royalist mint coinage was generally distrib-

The Bitterley Hoard. The coins were buried in a leather bag inside an earthenware pot. The individual coin shown was produced by the mint established by the Royalists at Bristol following the capture of the city in July 1643.

uted relatively locally, there is a strong possibility that the coins had been in the possession of a soldier whose unit had been based in the Bristol area in 1643/44. Van Gerris' unit would fit this criteria, with the individual concerned dying before he could recover his temporarily secreted 'hoard'.[18]

The worst of Van Gerris' activities seem to have been around the Much Wenlock area and the Corve valley. Sir Lewis Kirke, Governor of Bridgnorth, and himself no great respecter of civilian rights, refused Van Gerris and his men entry to the town.[19] His depredations were the trigger for what was to be the first outbreak of the 'clubmen' protests of the Civil War which would spread to several areas of England.

The 'clubmen' movement was an increasingly significant feature of the later stages of the war in several parts of the country. Bands of armed civilians, often led by local gentry and clergy, took up arms vowing to protect their homes against the depredations of both Royalists and Parliamentarians. They took their name from the agricultural implements and improvised weapons with which they were sometimes armed.

December saw the first clubmen outbreak. The rising, which was centred in the Clun and Purslow Hundreds, was led by the vicar of Bishop's Castle and Jeremy Powell, Richard Heath and Francis Harris – all minor local gentry – who reportedly gathered about 1,200 protesters. Their demands were not overtly political, being for the removal of Van Gerris, compensation for the money and other goods he had taken, and the evacuation of the new garrisons at Bishop's Castle and Lea Hall. Another protest group reportedly gathered at Leintwardine.

On 6 January 1645 the Parliamentarian newsletter, *Mercurius Britannicus*, reported:

> ... out of Shropshire we hear that there are about a thousand in arms about Clun and Bishop's Castle standing out against both sides, neither for the King nor for the Parliament, but standing up[on] their own guard for the preservation of their lives and fortunes. The occasion for this was the friendly usage which they received from His Majesty's officers in these parts particularly from one [Van Gerris]. They are absolutely resolved (notwithstanding all the entreaties used by the Commissioners of Array) not to lay down their arms unless His Majesty grant their conditions.[20]

Confusion was heightened by a parallel scheme which had its origins in a meeting held at Ludlow on 12 November by the Shropshire gentry. They resolved to write to Parliament in association with neighbouring counties, including Worcestershire, demanding that it should make peace with the king. In December the two counties agreed to raise a force of local troops to keep order and defend against Parliamentarian attacks. The origins of this particular movement lay in the king's 'One and All' proclamation of the previous autumn, when he had called upon the militia of the counties of south-west England to be mustered to keep out Parliamentarian forces. In the event, the idea aroused little enthusiasm and came to nothing. However in the Marches, where Royalist control was much less secure and enemy raiding much more prevalent, the idea seemed to meet with much greater support. The king and his commanders were cautious, knowing that any force raised and armed for local defence might equally well be used against Royalist troops, or even switch sides altogether. The demand that the association troops should be maintained by the income from sequestered [confiscated] Parliamentarian estates, which were currently used in the support of Royalist troops, was a major concern to the king's commanders. Whilst voicing cautious agreement with the scheme, the king required that any force raised should be commanded by officers provided by the Royalists.

As was inevitable, the local men mustered had little interest in the wider issues of the war, and became diverted into the neutralist clubmen movement, in effect opposed to both sides in the war.

The Shropshire clubmen had one of their demands met when, possibly as a result of Woodhouse's pleas, Van Gerris and his troublesome troopers were transferred elsewhere, though probably not before the end of 1644. (Van Gerris himself was killed in action at Lancaut in Monmouthshire in February 1645.) But this would not be the end of Woodhouse's problems.[21] With the garrisons at Stokesay and Lea Hall still maintained, the discontent of the clubmen continued and simmered on to some extent into the summer in the Bishop's Castle area.

On 3 January 1645 Sir Michael Ernley wrote to Prince Rupert from Shrewsbury, in connection with the Association proposed by the gentry, saying that:

> ... the disorders seen in this county made by the Gentlemen upon pretence of rectifying levies and drawing the carrying of the whole business into a form of their own contrary to your Highness's orders and instructions given to your highness's Commissioners or my Commission do so much increase that it hath encouraged the enemy to draw a great force into the country upon what design I know not but they were this very night within four miles of this Town, and hope to join with those gentlemen and seditious people in the Country who have mustered 3000 and do stop in the meanwhile all contributions from hence and the other garrisons so that I am in more danger of mutinies within than their force without.

The Association had been asked to support an establishment of 200 foot and 60 horse at Ludlow, to which they had reluctantly agreed, but Ernley expected 'nothing but confusion' from their other meetings.[22]

On 30 November 1644 Prince Rupert had been promoted to command the king's main army at Oxford. Rupert was replaced in north Wales and the Marches by his younger brother, Prince Maurice. Maurice has tended to receive critical treatment from both contemporaries and later writers. On the outbreak of the war he had lacked even Rupert's limited previous experience, but had gone on to prove a capable cavalry officer, and despite periods of ill-health had showed promise as an overall army commander. As it was, the current military position of the Royalists in the Welsh Marches would have tested an even more capable general.

In November the Cheshire Parliamentarians had commenced a blockade, or 'leaguer', of Chester, and by the middle of January the Royalist garrison there

Prince Maurice (1620-52). Though disliked by the king's civilian advisors because of his lack of finesse, he was a capable cavalry commander. He was hampered in the Marches by lack of resources and conflicting demands.

was under serious pressure. Maurice gathered a force to march to its relief, and in doing so stripped troops from a number of other garrisons, including Shrewsbury. Whilst Maurice operated ineffectively in the vicinity of Chester, the Shropshire Parliamentarians seized their chance, and on the night of 22 February stormed Shrewsbury in a surprise assault.

The loss of Shrewsbury was a devastating blow for the Cavaliers. At a stroke communications between the recruiting grounds of north Wales and the king's headquarters at Oxford were severed, and Chester was left further isolated. Ludlow, from being relatively secure Royalist territory, was now thrust into the front line. From Ludlow, Sir Michael Woodhouse wrote gloomily to Prince Rupert at noon on 22 February:

> A quarter of an hour since Sir Thomas Eyton came to this place and brought with him the sad news of the loss of Shrewsbury. The last night the enemy were let into the town, and he affirms that as the soldiers were repairing to their alarm places the Townsmen beat them down and took away their arms, he escaped over the water and can give no other particulars of this sad truth.
>
> I am here in a bad condition having a false people to deal with, and not of force, having sent 120 men with the Prince [Maurice], to fetch in provisions, which I want, having fed my men upon my magazine ever since this new rebellion. Yet by God's help, I will give your Highness an account within the Castle three months hence, the Town may be found in some disorder, for the people understand nothing but treachery. Prince Maurice is about Ruthin, God send him safe hither, with this I have sent an express to your Highness, and desire I may have ten barrels of powder from Worcester or Hereford, for I have not so many here …
>
> The country is in such a confusion with this association, that if you look not after this place I believe they will besiege it first and with this number if I quit the town they say they will keep me in [the Castle]. I am not above 200 men, the town can make 800 well armed.[23]

There is no evidence to confirm that Woodhouse's fears of rebellion within Ludlow were justified. Certainly there was discontent, and Sir Michael may have been thinking of a petition presented to him by the town bailiffs at around this time. Most of their complaints and requests were similar to those expressed by the civilian authorities in other garrison towns. They asked that provisions should only be demanded by a warrant from the governor, and payment be made according to the regulations laid down by Prince Rupert. Property within the town should be protected from plundering by soldiers, and those involved be punished by civilian Common Law, not by a military Council of War, which presumably was expected to be more lenient.

They protested that inhabitants were being turned out of their houses to provide quarters for soldiers, and demanded that no troops should be billeted on householders without the latter receiving payment for their keep. They also protested that they should not be required to pay towards the upkeep of soldiers quartered in the castle. It was probably some of Woodhouse's men quartered there who were accused of taking away 100 beds and other furniture from the town.[24]

The surviving evidence suggests that billets presented for expenses incurred by the garrison were normally paid with a fair amount of regularity. The problems arose when troops passing through the town were quartered briefly on civilians, who might then have trouble obtaining payment afterwards. Among a large number of surviving accounts submitted by civilians for costs incurred in billeting soldiers are the following relating to quartering Colonel Devalier's troop: Thomas Wellings £3 4s, William Powis £1 15s, Philip Starke £1 1s William Croweller £2 1s and William Aston £16 15s 6d.[25]

There is evidence that soldiers were also billeted in empty houses. A list of such houses, probably dating to 1645, survives in the bailiffs' papers and includes the following properties, the figures indicating the numbers of soldiers quartered:

Castle Ward
Ralph Godwin Esq (Castle Lodge) 5
Robert Berry gent. 10
Edward Wogan gent. 8
Mr Richard Gough 6
Thomas Roberts (4 Mill St) 4
Sir Adam Littleton 4
Harford's house 2
The Leaden Porch (16-18 Castle St) 6
Mr Goodwin, clerk 6
Thomas Cross (12 High Street) 6
Thomas Cross, more, 6
Mr Keyes house 5
Edward Jencks shop 5

Broad Street Ward
Mr John Sherman a house 4
Mr John Sherman another house 4
Mr Richard Hall 6
Mr Owens, clerk 8
Simon Webb 6
Edward Cook 5
John Cleobury 5
Mr Merrick for 'the Greyhound' (an inn at 49 Broad St) 8

Old Street Ward

Mr Fisher's tavern 5	William Hooler 3	
Mr Keye's house 5	Hugh Powell 4	
Mr Thomas Cam's house 2	Mr Egerton 5[26]	
Mr Rees Jones (the Feathers) 8		

The total of 150 soldiers so billeted, and allowing for some soldiers, perhaps as many as 100, being quartered in the castle, probably accounts for the bulk of the troops in Ludlow in the earlier part of 1645. Problems would increase later, as the survivors of various fragmented units began to arrive.

It was claimed in 1645 that billeting and supplying troops had cost the town a total of £850 17s 10d. Much of this had been repaid, including probably the cost of 'the maintenance of XXV trained soldiers above one whole year at 6s a week'. Other costs were not recompensed, however. Tradesmen supplied one group of soldiers with gunpowder, match, clothes, stockings, boots, shoes and other commodities to a value of £35 12s 3d, but were left unpaid. Some of Prince Rupert's Bluecoats failed to pay for £15 10s worth of 'horsemeat'.[27]

There were other grievances; a man who had already had three horses commandeered also had his spade requisitioned for work on the fortifications, leaving him with no means of tilling his garden, and with a wife, children and billeted soldier to support.[28]

As Royalist-controlled territory shrank, so Sir Michael Woodhouse became more exacting in his efforts to raise money and supplies. Even though London was in Parliamentarian hands, by tacit agreement the Welsh had been allowed to continue the cattle trade so vital to their livelihoods. One of the cattle drovers' roads from north Wales passed through Ludlow to the Midlands and London. But on 29 January 1645, John Williams, Archbishop of York, now in north Wales, wrote to Prince Rupert:

> I humbly crave your Highness' favour to receive the Petition of our poor Drovers, which bring hither the little gold and silver we have) against the oppression of Sir Michael Wood-house.[29]

Williams likened the trade to the Spanish fleets which carried the gold of the New World to Spain. It is unlikely, however, that the petition, presumably protesting at the high tolls imposed on the drovers, met with a sympathetic response.

As the flow of supplies and money to Ludlow became ever harder to achieve, on 21 January Richard Wicksted and his neighbours wrote to Sir Francis Ottley from the town, appealing for his support in a dispute as to whether the financial contributions assessed for Condover Hundred by the Royalist authorities in the county should be paid to Ludlow 'upon which order we are detained, and without the payment of the money (which we cannot do) we have no hope of liberty'. But if Ottley could support him in his claim that the contribution had already been paid, to Bridgnorth, 'it seemeth by some whom I have used to sound Sir Michael Woodhouse, that he will not demand the same twice, if I have paid you'.[30]

The following day Wicksted wrote again that:

> ... it is feared that the hundred of Condover will be called upon to make up the sum of £200 which Sir Michael Woodhouse saith he hath lent to Prince Maurice, and had power given him to levy it upon the Country. But I see no order for it, nor when it is to be levied; if anywhere it is probable that it is to be done in those places which are under the contribution of Ludlow, which Condover Hundred never was. Any pretence will serve to charge us, and to keep us poor.[31]

William Bedoe of Ludlow would lodge a bill of complaint with the Chancery Court after the war, concerning a dispute over house and land ownership. It may well be, in this case at least, that certain individuals were trying to use the prevailing conditions as a mask to cause problems to their business rivals. Bedoe claimed that on 20 April 1645 a number of people 'with the aid of Charles Goodwin, Clerk, who had a hand in all the illegal proceedings, ... caused me to be imprisoned for a bankrupt in the marshall's ward of Ludlow when the king's army was in these parts where I remained a prisoner from 3 August to 18 August while they tried to force me to relinquish the tenancy etc.' Once released, Bedoe was forced to flee from Ludlow until the end of the war, when he thought his troubles were over. However on returning, he was re-arrested, and 'put into a loathsome place where the soldiers had their guard'. He had to pay large sums for his defence in the town court, 'and my clock was taken to pay costs'.[32]

On the whole, however, civic life continued in a fairly regular way. The council continued to meet, and to deal with day to day matters. There was, of course, an underlying anxiety regarding the effects of the war, which could sometimes be expressed in the treatment accorded to those seen as being Parliamentarian in sympathy. One man, Edward Vernon, would claim after the war that he had been imprisoned in Ludlow Castle until he paid the Royalists £50 as the price of his release.[33] The warden of the Thomas Brome Hospital at Clun claimed that in 1645 he was seized by the Royalists and taken to Ludlow, and then involved in a costly and involved effort to recover the deeds of the Hospital, which had also been seized by the Royalists.[34]

Also encountering problems was Humphrey Walcot of Clun, a minor landowner best described as a half-hearted Royalist. He made a number of contributions to the king in the opening years of the war, but clearly his loyalty was suspect, for 'since Shrewsbury was reduced Humphrey Walcot was taken from his house prisoner to Ludlow, and there detained until he ransomed himself with a good sum of money'.[35]

7 ROYALIST REVERSES

The military reverses suffered by the Royalists in the Marches in the early spring of 1645 led to Prince Rupert's personal intervention. There was now renewed restiveness from clubmen in south Shropshire, as Sir Barnabas Scudamore, Governor of Hereford, informed Prince Rupert on 3 March: 'What Shropshire hath done, I suppose your Highness knows, now they are rising to beat out sir William Vaughan's horse which his highness Prince Maurice hath sent to Ludlow for the defence of those parts. Their design is not to pay contribution nor to [accept] quarter.'[1] The affair will have done little to ease growing animosity between Woodhouse and Vaughan. Rupert was in Ludlow a few days later, accompanied by the Royalist commander for the East Midlands, Lord Loughborough, and Lord Astley, Major-General of Foot in the Oxford army. Here he received the news of the victory obtained by Sir Marmaduke Langdale and the Northern Horse on 2 March at Pontefract where Langdale relieved the garrison and routed the besiegers.[2] Having, apparently, conscripted some of the rebellious clubmen, and reinforced by Langdale and troops from the Oxford army, Rupert went on to unite his disparate force with that of Prince Maurice and relieve Chester. He then marched back to suppress a clubmen uprising in Herefordshire and to 'refresh after the Dutch fashion' as he put it, meaning that men, money and supplies were levied as in conquered territory. In April the entire male population of Herefordshire were required to take an oath of loyalty, on pain of being conscripted into the Royalist forces if they refused.[3]

Probably as a result of Rupert's visit and the discontent in the area, Ludlow's defences were strengthened. Woodhouse's pleas for gunpowder had been answered on 26 March when ten barrels arrived in a convoy from Worcester, part of a consignment of 36 which had been sent there from the mills in Bristol.[4] On 21 April a Parliamentarian spy reported from an outlying village to Sir William Brereton in Cheshire:

> They are pulling down the gates in Ludlow [perhaps to replace them] and making works on the north side of the Castle. They sent warrants to the constables to bring ten pioneers out of our allotment, but we have sent but two in. How we shall speed the Lord knows.[5]

By early May, as the king prepared to take the field for his summer campaign, the clubmen movement in Shropshire and Herefordshire had been crushed. Once again some of the garrisons in the Marches were called upon to provide reinforcements for the king's army, but although Woodhouse was called to a meeting with the king and other local commanders on 15 May at Cofton, near Droitwich, he was not required to detach any of the Ludlow garrison.[6] There was good reason for this, for the Parliamentarians were drawing uncomfortably close to Ludlow.

The departure of many troops from the remaining Royalist garrisons in Shropshire to reinforce the king's field army presented the still weak Shropshire Parliamentarians, based now in Shrewsbury, with an opportunity to take the offensive. Early in June:

> There was drawn out of this Garrison by order from the Committee, 500 foot and 300 horse, viz: part of Colonel Mackworth's Regiment, and part of Colonel Lloyd's Regiment, both of these marched along in the service; our Forces marched within five miles of Ludlow, the design being to reduce that part of the country; and to secure it by placing some garrisons there to block up Ludlow. We sent Lieutenant-Colonel Reinking [a Dutch professional soldier] to view Stokesay Castle, a garrison of the enemie's; the place was conceived considerable, therefore the next morning we drew up to it, and summoned it, but the Governor Captain [Gerard] Dannet [of Woodhouse's regiment] refused; thereupon we prepared for a storm; being ready to fall on, we gave a second summons, which was hearkened unto, a parley admitted, and the Castle delivered up and is now garrisoned by us.[7]

Dannet, heavily outnumbered, had decided it was better to take his men back to Ludlow to fight another day rather than be slaughtered in a hopeless defence.

Reinking's force was intended to operate in the area of Corvedale, between Bridgnorth and Ludlow, in order to cut communications between those two places. They planned to occupy the recently abandoned minor Royalist outposts of Holgate and Broncroft Castle. Holgate was found to have been too thoroughly demolished to be defensible, but a garrison, commanded by Lord Calvin, was established at Broncroft Castle.

Stokesay Castle c.1900s. (Ridgebourne Archives)

The Parliamentarian operations presented a threat which Woodhouse could not ignore, although his own troops at Ludlow were too weak to counterattack alone. In order to raise an effective field force, Sir Michael called for reinforcements from a wide area. They included detachments from the garrisons at Monmouth, Worcester and Hereford, under their respective governors, Sir Thomas Lunsford, Sir Samuel Sandys and Barnabas Scudamore, together with Sir William Sandys, the commander of a small Royalist field army in Worcestershire. The Herefordshire troops included what remained of the regiment of Sir William Croft. The various contingents joined Woodhouse at Ludlow, giving him a total of around 2,000 horse and foot. The Royalists left Ludlow on 8 June, their main objective being to recover Stokesay Castle. They initially induced Lord Calvin to abandon Broncroft Castle without a fight, and then swung south towards Stokesay.

Learning of the Royalists' approach, Reinking withdrew the bulk of his men about one and a half miles to the north, leaving the castle garrisoned, and awaited reinforcements from Montgomery and Shrewsbury. The Royalists decided to seize the moment and advanced to the attack. The action which followed is usually known as the Battle of Wistanstow, but the evidence of skeletons uncovered in the 19th century indicates that the main fighting probably occurred in the vicinity of Whettleton Bank.

When their scouts reported the Royalist advance, the Parliamentarian commanders called a hasty council of war. Opinion was divided: Reinking favoured retreat, but Colonels Mackworth and Lloyd, with their second in commands, Majors Roger Fenwick and Anthony Hungerford, persuaded him to stand and fight, despite a Royalist numerical superiority of around two to one. In fact, the Royalists were labouring under their own disadvantages. Nobody seems to have been in undisputed command of their collection of detachments from several garrisons, who in many cases were unaccustomed to working together. Leading a battle by committee is never conducive to success, as would now be demonstrated.

Few details of the action survive, with none from the Royalist viewpoint. The one Parliamentarian account suggests that the Royalists lined the hedgerows of the lane leading to the Parliamentarian position with their musketeers, then advanced a party of their cavalry to attack, possibly with the intention of tempting the enemy into an ambush as the result of a rash counterattack. The Parliamentarian horse, evidently in somewhat piecemeal fashion, engaged the Royalist advance party:

> Our horse made what haste they could to fight in. Captain ffoulkes' troop, to which were joined some reformadoes, fell upon a body of the enemy's horse, being 200, and routed them, after whom the foot marched on with gallant resolution, beat up all their ambuscadoes in the hedges for a mile together until they came to the main body, which after an hour's fight was routed and dispersed. In this business Colonel Reinking deserves much honour, as much as a man could do, and also the other colonels did very gallantly. We slew near 100 upon the place, took 300 common soldiers, about 80 officers and gentlemen, and all their ordnance, bag and baggage, 4 barrels of powder, a good quantity of match and bullet, 100 horse, some gentlemen of quality were slain, these being the most of the gallantry of Herefordshire. In the action Sir William Croft, the best head piece and activist man in that county was slain on the place, the Governors of Monmouth and Ludlow hardly escaped, Sir Michael Woodhouse his horse being taken. Major Fenwick who behaved himself most gallantly is wounded but we hope not mortally.[8]

According to tradition, Sir William Croft escaped from the battlefield, but was pursued and killed as he approached Croft Castle.

Taken as prisoners were Colonel James Broughton, Captains Walter Neale, George Wright, Thomas Stot, Captain-Lieutenant Joseph Singe, two cornets, three ensigns, two lieutenants, three sergeants, nine quartermasters, seven corporals, five waggoners, three matrosses (gun crew), Gerald Steele (physician) and Richard Richardson (surgeon). The Royalists may also have had four light guns, or drakes, captured.[9] Some entries in the burial register of St Laurence's Ludlow may also relate to the action, notably Roger Rudge and Robert Oldham, two soldiers named as being buried on 7 and 16 June respectively.[10]

The action near Stokesay was a major disaster for the Royalists in the southern Marches. Woodhouse was now forced largely on the defensive and would make no further attempts to recover Stokesay Castle; it remained firmly in Parliamentarian hands for the remainder of the war.

Within a few days of his defeat, news will have reached Sir Michael of the effective destruction of the king's Oxford army at the Battle of Naseby on 14 June. Although the war had a year or more still to run, Royalist hopes grew steadily bleaker.

News of Naseby, and locally of the defeat at Stokesay, resulted in the surrender of Caus Castle, north-west of Ludlow on the Welsh Border. This had been held for the king by John Devalier, but in late June the Parliamentarians laid siege to the castle, and on the 25th, as the besiegers were preparing to storm the castle, Devalier and his men surrendered. They handed over all ammunition and powder, and 'with their colours and swords only', were given 'safe convoy to the King's next garrison'.[11]

This was Ludlow, and Devalier and his men formed a useful addition to Woodhouse's garrison. They evidently included a number of foreign troops, possibly some of them Irish, although the surrender terms at Caus had denied this. In any event, they were hardened soldiers who would have little sympathy with civilian grievances, and Woodhouse apparently used them to garrison the castle, his intended final refuge in case of insurrection by the townspeople.

Despite the heavy defeat at Wistanstow, Ludlow did not yet come under direct attack. There were a number of reasons for this. Royalist forces in the southern Marches remained relatively strong, and the Shropshire Parliamentarian committee had been required to despatch the bulk of its troops to assist the Cheshire Parliamentarians in the difficult task of capturing Chester. There seemed likely to be no speedy end to this siege, and so Woodhouse was left in relative peace.

Musketeer. The soldier depicted here wears the mixture of civilian dress which was common, particularly at the end of a campaigning season.

On 9 July King Charles, with some of his remaining cavalry, arrived at Ludlow, and remained until the next day. From the castle he issued a number of orders to raise new recruits. None of them came to much, as by now it was proving increasingly difficult to obtain conscripts from the hostile population.[12] The king moved on to Raglan in south Wales, and during August the main concern in the area was the arrival of Parliament's Scottish allies in Herefordshire, where they laid siege to Hereford itself. However the king gained almost his final success of the war, when he led a relief force which caused the Scots to raise the siege and withdraw north-wards.[13]

Soon after the Scots withdrew, the Ludlow horse co-operated with Sir Barnabas Scudamore, Governor of Hereford, in an unsuccessful attempt to regain the outpost at Canon Frome which the Scots had captured in their advance on Hereford, massacring the garrison. The Parliamentarian Shropshire horse struck back with a raid as far as the suburbs of Ludlow, causing alarm, but not seriously threatening the town.[14]

The Ludlow horse, meanwhile, were continuing to mount foraging expeditions into the neighbouring area, and on 25 August one of these came to grief, as the Parliamentarian Shropshire Committee reported:

> It hath pleased God to give us a further evidence of his goodness by delivering into our hands 140 of the enemie's forces belonging unto Ludlow, who amongst others to the number of 300 were sent under the command of Colonel Devalier towards Bishop's Castle to plunder the country. After some hurt done, our forces consisting of 80 horse and 80 foot, under the command of Major Fenwick, which quartered in Bishop's Castle for securing that town and parts adjacent, drew forth, and within a mile of that place, with the assistance of some countrymen that were got into a body, charged the enemy. Our forlorn [advance party of] foot soldiers retreated disorderly, but our horse did second them so gallantly, that, after a hot charge, they wholly routed the enemy, brought off all the prisoners to the number above specified, whereof almost 20 were commissioned officers, and we are credibly informed that there came not above 40 back to Ludlow, besides those which were brought back wounded in carts.[15]

Casualty figures are generally untrustworthy and there are no entries in the Ludlow Burial Registers that clearly relate to this action. It was certainly not the end of the raids by the Ludlow horse, but must have been a significant reverse for them.

For now the main efforts by the Royalists on the Welsh Border were focused on attempts to relieve pressure on Chester under siege again since the suburbs were surprised by the Parliamentarians on 21 September. King Charles with all the horse he could muster marched northwards in September, but on 25 September suffered a serious defeat outside Chester at the Battle of Rowton Heath. There is nothing to suggest that any Ludlow units were present on this occasion. Indeed, on 18 September, a Royalist officer, Robert Howard, wrote from Bridgnorth to the king's Secretary of State, Lord George Digby:

> … the country is so far under the control of the rebels, that there is no safe place of meeting but in the garrisons of Bridgnorth and Ludlow, where, from what I observe we may expect rather opposition than furtherance.[16]

The king himself headed across the Midlands to Newark, leaving Sir William Vaughan, with an extensive commission as Major-General of Horse, to continue to co-ordinate efforts to relieve Chester. Vaughan's background is obscure, though he was evidently a pupil of Shrewsbury School and most probably kin to the numerous Vaughans of the Herefordshire/Radnorshire border. He was a hard-bitten veteran of the war in Ireland, and since returning with his regiment of horse in the spring of 1644, had gained a fearsome reputation along the Welsh Border. According to one Royalist account he was known to the Shropshire Parliamentarians as 'The Devil of Shrawardine', having his main stronghold at Shrawardine Castle near Shrewsbury. Vaughan was very much in the 'warlord' mould, running his network of north Shropshire garrisons virtually as a private fiefdom. Woodhouse had co-operated with Vaughan on occasion, sending him troops to help regain High Ercall House in April, but with Shrawardine lost in June, Vaughan and the extremely piecemeal and fragmentary collection of units under his command seem to have been quartered mainly around Bridgnorth and Much Wenlock. Not only were they undisciplined, they competed with Woodhouse and Sir Lewis Kirke at Bridgnorth for quarters, provisions and contributions. Unsurprisingly these features would prove to be increasing sources of friction and dispute.[17]

Chester remained the over-riding concern of the Royalists in the region, and during October Vaughan desperately scraped together troops from the Marcher garrisons for another relief attempt. This time Woodhouse provided a contingent. At Stokesay, the Parliamentarian governor, Major Anthony Hungerford, kept close watch on Royalist activities, and reported on 25 October:

> As I wrote to you yesterday … I was not deceived in the enemy's quartering last night at Presteigne. I sent a party of but six men with firelocks to molest them with an alarm, which they gave them to purpose, and took five prisoners with their arms in their quarters, one of Vaughan's troopers and four Worcester footmen. They gave this relation: that there are more than 3,000, and most of them horse, that Vaughan is with them and [Henry] Washington [Governor of Worcester] and they think [Charles] Gerard. It was spoken amongst them yesterday that Prince Maurice was expected, that they are designed to raise a siege, but where they know not. This is all I can get from them.

That same night another party of Hungerford's men 'fetched' from Ludlow Thomas Crowther, who had been elected High Bailiff in October 1644 after which he and the Low Bailiff, Edward Turford, were two members of a six-man committee chosen to represent the town council in dealing with assessments and other military demands on the town. 'So you may think they get it [the demands] with much difficulty'.[18]

Vaughan and his force marched north along the border, and then to Denbigh, where they hoped to be joined by Royalist troops from north Wales before attempting the relief of Chester. On 28 October, Samuel More, now Parliamentarian governor of Montgomery, reported:

> Sir William Vaughan commanded the party. With him was Washington, Grady, [Randolph] Egerton, who came from Carmarthen with his own and some of [Roger] Whitley's horse; 100 firelocks of Prince Maurice from Worcester; some horse and foot from Hereford; Captain Deane from Ludlow with 80 foot and some of Devalier's horse.[19]

In a separate report, Richard Symonds said there were 90 of Woodhouse's foot present, evidently one company.[20]

On 1 November Vaughan's force was brought to battle on Denbigh Green, just outside Denbigh itself, by a Parliamentarian force drawn from the besiegers of Chester. The Royalists were routed, and although Vaughan and the bulk of his troops escaped, a number of prisoners were taken. They included the following members of the Ludlow garrison: Lewis Davies, Henry Powell and Henry Lingard from Woodhouse's regiment; Humphrey Redditch from Devalier's regiment; and Edward Morgan, a trooper from either Woodhouse's or Devalier's regiment.[21]

The Ludlow garrison had meanwhile been taking advantage of the absence of many of the Shropshire Parliamentarian forces at Chester, for on 3 November the Shropshire Parliamentarian committee complained to Sir William Brereton that 'the long absence of our horse hath so encouraged the enemy at Ercall, Bridgnorth and Ludlow garrisons that they continually infest us on every side.T.hey asked for the return of as many of their cavalry as could be spared.[22]

Despite these sparks of defiance, the defeat at Denbigh Green would prove to be the death blow to Sir William Vaughan's attempts to relieve Chester. His troops either returned to their garrisons or spread out across the southern marches, raiding and plundering, and incurring mounting local opposition, whilst the Royalist garrison commanders bickered amongst themselves. The clubmen of south-west Shropshire were now effectively allied with the Parliamentarians in their resistance to Royalist raiders.

The combination of events meant that relations between Sir Michael Woodhouse and Vaughan sank to new depths. In December Sir William Brereton received reports that the Royalists were mustering at Ludlow for a new attempt to relieve Chester. But, Woodhouse, sharing the opinion of a local Parliamentarian that Vaughan's disorderly cavalry were 'the most rude, ravenous and ill-governed horse that I believe ever trod upon the Earth', and unwilling to share supplies, refused them admittance to the town.[23] Others of the potential relief force seemed in poor shape; it was reported to Brereton that 'some small numbers daily pass from Worcester towards Bewdley and Ludlow. They are merely ragged and ravenous troops and will never march to the rendezvous where service is never intended.'[24]

As relations between Woodhouse and Vaughan continued to sour, there were even reports that the two men were about to fight a duel. Whether true or not, it is unlikely that Sir Michael displayed any great sympathy when a party of Vaughan's men suffered a reverse at Church Stoke Church. According to the Parliamentarian newspaper *Free Informer* of 14 February 1646:

> A party of Sir William Vaughan's horse on the side of the King, marched through a great part of Shropshire, plundering as they went. They went from Clun to Knighton, and Presteigne, thence by Brampton Bryan and over Leintwardine Bridge were proceeding towards Ludlow; but being closely pursued by Captain Marvin, they were forced to take sanctuary in Stoke Church, into which they got some of their horse, and stood upon their guard. Before they got into the Church, we had a sharp conflict with them, which put them to the rout, and killed a Captain, Lieutenant, and others, and took some prisoners. This being near Ludlow, it is doubted [expected] the enemy will receive relief in the Church, but they will heed how they strangle again so far.

The *Cittie's Weekly Post* (another Parliamentarian journal) of 16-17 February 1646 gave further details:

> We understood from Wales that Sir William Vaughan expecting to be besieged at High Ercall by some of Sir William Brereton's forces who were lately before Chester, did send out a strong party to bring in provisions to maintain them if the place should be besieged, and to levy contributions, and to take what prisoners they could, intending if they were persons of estate that they should purchase their deliverance, either by ransoms or exchange. Having received these orders, this plundering party marched to Clun, and so near unto Stokesay, that the Governor of it receiving the alarm in time, sallied forth against them with a considerable strength, and having followed them seven miles, our forlorn hope at length overtook them, and set on their party, which immediately did fly towards their main body, where they grew so bold as to stand still awhile, and to look our forces in the face; but finding that we were resolved to encounter with them, and came up in good equipage to perfect that resolution, they obeyed again the ignominious counsel of their fears, and fled from the field to take sanctuary in a church; but before they could arrive unto it, we slew three or four of their men, took divers prisoners, amongst which were some of note and quality. They had no sooner entered the church, but the alarm was brought to Ludlow, and notice given in what danger they were if sudden relief was not sent unto them; whereupon a strong party of horse immediately was drawn forth for their rescue, but our men understanding of their coming, and being wearied with their long march, and the ill ways made more heavy by the thaw which more deeply did corrupt them, they retreated back, having not one man slain, nor one man wounded in this service.[25]

On 16 December the staggering Royalist cause in the southern Marches suffered another crushing blow when Parliamentarian troops led by Colonel John Birch captured Hereford in a surprise attack. The Governor, Sir Barnabas Scudamore, managed to escape over the walls and carried the news of his defeat to Ludlow.

The loss of Hereford meant that Ludlow might now also be threatened from the south, and precautions were taken. On 23 December it was reported to Sir William Brereton that troops from Ludlow had burnt Croft Castle, some 10 miles south-west of the town. With Sir William Croft dead, Woodhouse's main concern was that the castle might be used as a base by the Parliamentarians.[26]

The winter of 1645-46 was harsh. In besieged Chester the Welsh troops of the garrison huddled in straw in their quarters in an attempt to keep warm, and the River Dee was frozen over. Roads were clogged with snow, and with Shrewsbury in Parliamentarian hands, its garrison prevented supplies of coal reaching Bridgnorth and Ludlow, adding to the miseries of the inhabitants who were already burdened with increasing numbers of Royalist refugees from elsewhere and various fragmented and disorderly military units.[27]

The problems caused by the weather did not prevent Colonel John Devalier from continuing his demands on the surrounding communities. On 22 January Thomas Edwards wrote to Sir Francis Ottley, now in Bridgnorth:

> I have solicited daily to have his [Devalier's] Warrants sent forth, but to this hour cannot get them. He shuffles it to the Governor that he doth oppose them as a hindrance to his contributions, and yet I call upon him and have promised that he will collect the money and use the first that comes in.[28]

In a last-ditch attempt to restore order in the Marches and somehow relieve Chester, on 6 December the king had appointed Lord Astley as Lieutenant-General of Worcestershire, Herefordshire, Shropshire and Staffordshire. Astley was a vastly experienced and competent soldier who had commanded the foot of the Oxford army throughout the war until the defeat at Naseby. But by now the chaotic Royalist cause was beyond redemption, though Astley did his best. He brought Vaughan's men under some kind of control, and reorganised the remaining garrisons as well as he could. Hindered first by snow, then by flooded rivers when the thaw came, by the end of January Astley had mustered a field force of about 2,000 horse and 1,500 foot with which to make a last desperate attempt to save Chester. But he was too late; on 3 February, faced with riot and mutiny by starving citizens and soldiers, Lord Byron surrendered the city to Sir William Brereton.

King Charles clung to one last desperate hope. Astley was ordered to add to his field army every man who

Jacob, Lord Astley (1579-1652).
A man of few words, Astley was a highly competent
professional soldier and Major General of Foot in
the Royalist Oxford army for most of the war.
He was placed in command of the remaining
Royalist forces in the Marches in December 1645,
tasked with the relief of Chester and raising
a new field army.

could be spared from the few remaining Royalist garrisons, and march to join the king near Oxford. By the middle of March he had mustered around 3,000 men, and set off on his desperate mission.

With Parliamentarian forces under Brereton, Birch from Hereford and Morgan from Gloucester closing in, Astley showed some skill in getting as far as he did. But the outcome was probably inevitable. On 21 March Astley was brought to bay at Stow on the Wold in the Cotswolds, and the last Royalist field army was overwhelmed. Sitting on a drum among his captors, Astley commented, 'You have done your work, boys, and may go play, unless you fall out among yourselves.' It is unclear whether any Ludlow troops were in Astley's little army. None of their officers are identifiable among the prisoners, but there are modern references to Devalier having been captured in March, and escaping, so that could well have happened at Stow. There is certainly no mention of him in Ludlow after this time.[29]

At Ludlow, Woodhouse and Devalier's horse had remained active into the New Year. On 21 January a Parliamentarian commander reported to the speaker of the House of Commons: 'Raglan and Ludlow horse prove very prejudicial and much infest our friends within their reach'.

But for the few remaining Royalist garrisons, the reckoning was near. Some, knowing the war to be lost, surrendered. A few, like the defenders of Bridgnorth, fought desperately, with much of the town consumed in the flames before the garrison of the castle eventually surrendered on 24 April.

It remained to be seen what Sir Michael Woodhouse at Ludlow, the last remaining Royalist garrison in Shropshire, would do.

8 THE SIEGE OF LUDLOW

As he surveyed his prospects, Sir Michael Woodhouse had few promising options. An experienced professional soldier, he would have realised that the defeat at Stow on the Wold meant that the Royalist cause was irrevocably lost. There was no longer any viable army left to the king. His remaining garrisons were surrendering or being picked off, one by one. Ludlow, as the last surviving unbesieged Royalist garrison in Shropshire, was clearly doomed. Charles himself was about to seek refuge with his Scottish foes in an attempt to divide his opponents. Woodhouse's own political views are unclear. He was probably not one of the most ardent of Cavaliers, but on the other hand he evidently never considered serving Parliament.

There were, however, sound reasons deterring him from simply surrendering. Like other professional soldiers in the king's service, Woodhouse would have been considering future employment prospects. These would lie in the continuing fighting on the Continent, and it was important that he should be able to demonstrate to future prospective employers his determination and resolution. Such thoughts would encourage him to put up at least a reasonable show of resistance, as would a reason closer to home. With the 'massacre' at Hopton Castle still a burning issue, Woodhouse had good reason to fear falling into the hands of the Shropshire Parliamentarians, who might well exact summary justice. Though he must have known that eventual surrender was inevitable, Woodhouse would have been determined that it should be on terms which guaranteed his own safety.

To defend Ludlow, Woodhouse had about 250 foot, probably men of his own regiment, and 100 horse, presumably the remains of Devalier's regiment together with other fragmentary units and 'reformadoes' – officers whose original units had been disbanded. He also had around 600 armed townsmen and other civilian refugees. But as Woodhouse knew, they had little appetite for a fight to the death – any more, in fact, than he did himself.

As for the besieging force, with the bulk of the Shropshire Parliamentarian forces tied down with the siege of Bridgnorth until well into April, Parliament gave the task of capturing Ludlow to John Birch, Governor of Hereford. On 10 April he was told:

> We desire you with all your horse and the foot belonging to Hereford, besides such forces as are coming to your assistance from cos. Salop, Montgomery and Radnor, forthwith to march to Ludlow and make what improvement you can of them for the reducing and taking in of that garrison.[1]

The keep at Ludlow Castle. During the latter stages of Ludlow's occupation by the Royalists the castle was garrisoned by men of Sir Michael Woodhouse's regiment of foot or John Devalier's regiment of horse. Woodhouse was concerned to ensure that the castle, which might be his final refuge, was held by men not linked with the townspeople.

The same day the county committees of Montgomery, Radnorshire and Shropshire were ordered

> To supply 200 foot, if they can spare them to aid Colonel Birch in the taking of Ludlow, and to enable him the better to effect that work. Send to such rendezvous as he shall appoint what force of horse and foot of your county you can possibly spare for that service. Certify us speedily what forces you will send him.[2]

John Birch was born in 1615 to a Lancashire family. His parents were strongly Presbyterian in religious belief, though it is not clear that Birch believed with the same enthusiasm. Before the outbreak of the Civil War, he was a successful wine merchant in Bristol, but lost his property and fortune when the Royalists stormed the city in July 1643. As much out of the hope that Parliament would compensate him for his losses as from political conviction, Birch joined the Parliamentarian forces. He proved a capable soldier, becoming a cavalry colonel, though from the start of his career he was noted as neglecting 'no opportunity of providing for himself'. After the Second Battle of Newbury, in October 1644, Birch captured the coach carrying the elderly wife of the Royalist general, the Earl of Forth, and their valuables. The lady was returned, but after Birch's death, some of the Forths' silver plate was found amongst his effects! Birch served with Parliament's New Model Army in the West of England, and was made Governor of Bristol on its recapture. His greatest exploit, however had been his capture of Hereford in the previous December, and he was appointed as its governor.[3]

For Sir Michael Woodhouse, the fact that Birch was commanding his besiegers was a piece of good fortune: he would have realised that the pragmatic Birch was much more likely than the Shropshire Parliamentarians to grant him favourable terms. Nevertheless, it was still necessary to at least go through the motions of resisting, however unfortunate that might be for the civilian population caught up in the proceedings.

Birch himself anticipated that Ludlow would be 'easily persuaded to yield upon good terms', which might indeed have been the case if Samuel More had not been present with the besiegers.

Birch appeared before Ludlow on Friday 24 April. He had with him around 350 horse and 660 foot. Of these, 450 foot and 250 horse were his own Hereford forces, 150 Shropshire foot and a troop of horse under Samuel More, and 60 foot and 40 horse from Radnorshire. The Parliamentarians do not seem to have had any artillery with them, certainly no heavy guns.[4]

Woodhouse had already begun demolishing some of the suburbs in preparation for a siege. Houses on the eastern side of Corve Street, below the town walls, had been cleared by October 1645, for on 31 October the corporation had ordered that 'the Bailiffs and surveyors should survey the demolished houses in Corve Street and set meen stones [presumably boundary markers] between the properties'. Some buildings in Castle Square had also been cleared.[5]

With attack now imminent, Woodhouse appreciated that he lacked sufficient manpower to attempt to hold the suburbs. These and the outer works which had been built were therefore to be abandoned and the defence concentrated on the town walls and castle. The Royalists now had little time in which to clear buildings from near the outside of the town walls which would have provided cover for attackers – unless buildings could be systematically demolished by teams of workmen, the only ways in which they could be removed was either by fire or gunpowder. Woodhouse almost certainly

John Birch (1616-91). A pragmatic Lancashire Presbyterian, Birch became a successful Bristol merchant, joining the Parliamentarian forces after the capture of the city by the Royalists in July 1643. Noted for his acquisitive nature, Birch was frequently accused, with some justice, of taking advantage of any financial opportunities which presented themselves.

had insufficient gunpowder to spare any for demolition purposes, so he attempted to fire the remaining suburbs using either fire arrows, the method employed by Lord Byron at Chester in 1645, or by setting fire to them by means of burning torches. Using either method successfully still required both time and manpower, for even thatched buildings could sometimes be difficult to set alight. It is unlikely that the townspeople would have provided more than half-hearted assistance and they may in fact have been deliberately obstructive, meaning the task would probably have had to be undertaken by Woodhouse's own men. As we shall see, although the Parliamentarians claimed to have disrupted the operation and saved most of the suburbs, the available evidence indicates that the Royalists did cause considerable destruction along Nether and Upper Galdeford, Corve Street about as far north as St Leonards, Linney, and Lower Broad Street, with more destruction, albeit on a smaller scale, in Mill and Old Streets. Possibly only Lower Corve Street escaped intended destruction.[6]

As the Parliamentarian force advanced, there was limited skirmishing in the ruins of the suburbs. A Parliamentarian newsletter reported on 6 May that Birch:

> ... with some skirmishing forced the Enemy into the town and saved most of the suburbs which the Enemy would have fired, hath made a formidable Leaguer, was faced with some forces of Raglan Goodrich and Maesfield [Madresfield, near Malvern] on Wednesday the 29th, who retreated. 60 horse are sent to convey the guns from Gloucester. A summons was sent in and a feasible answer returned, and there are within about 250 foot and 100 horse … in the town and castle. The horse made attempts to break away but were still forced back into the garrison. Colonel Birch (if not disturbed as is probable) will soon take Ludlow and reduce the Neighbour Garrisons also.[7]

Birch himself reported that 'I have laid close siege to Ludlow and doubt not, but to give such an account of it considering the shortness of the time I have been before it and the strength of the place may be expected of me …'.[8]

The summons that Birch 'sent in' to Woodhouse was couched in moderate terms:

> Gentlemen it is far from my desire to be an occasion of shedding of blood or ruining the estates of any. And for that I conceive yourselves are sensible of the danger of both…. It is yet in my power to prevent your own total ruin and in my power to grant you such terms as may be honourable to the Military part and profitable to those who have other resolutions than to live by their swords … there being neither any visible force in the Field nor any Garrison unbesieged which can yield you the least hopes of relief … To make miserable by refusing the opportunity offered [to avoid the consequences of an assault on the town]. For an example of the latter you need not send far to find those who have not only to their great dishonour destroyed utterly those under their protection, but have now thankfully within a few days embraced such terms as that their lives are at the Parliament's mercy, their own unadvisedness having been such that they had very near made the Besiegers incapable of granting them … incapable of giving you that which I now offer that all kind of misery follow which the sword necessarily brings with it. Your loving friend J. Birch from my leaguer 2 April 1646 [sic]. Answer by tomorrow by 12 of the clock and in the meantime if you desire it all acts of hostility shall be forborne on behalf of J.B.

Woodhouse was not yet quite ready to give up the game. He replied saying that he could not find 'any honour [in surrendering] without receiving His Majesty's command'. He was careful however to qualify this, by adding 'if extremity be made choice of I shall willingly condescend to what may void it as befits a soldier'.[9]

It is often assumed that the Parliamentarians employed artillery in the siege of Ludlow. The trench-like hollows on Whitcliffe Common have been suggested as being gun positions for Birch's siege guns, but they are more likely to be natural features. With this in mind, it is worth quoting the relevant contemporary letters. On 15 April the Committee of Both Kingdoms in London wrote as follows to the Parliamentarian committee in Gloucester:

> We have appointed Colonel Birch with some forces to endeavour the taking in of Ludlow, for which he will require some pieces of battery ordnance. He informs us that there are divers pieces at Gloucester that may be spared fit for that work.. We desire you to send him three whole culverins, with their equipage and ball, that he may be enabled to go through with that work.[10]

On 4 May they wrote a follow up letter:

> We wrote on the 13th [sic] to you to send three whole culverins with their equipage to Colonel Birch at Ludlow; this you may now omit to do, as we have thought fit to recall him to the place of his charge in Herefordshire, leaving the taking in of Ludlow to the forces of Salop. Retain the three culverins at Gloucester until further order.[11]

The pragmatist Birch would have probably quickly appreciated that Woodhouse was only, in modern parlance, 'going through the motions' and that there was no need to resort to a costly and destructive bombardment and assault on the town. The Committee of Both Kingdoms had, however, been made aware that in the absence of most of the Herefordshire forces, the Royalist garrison of Goodrich Castle, under Colonel Sir Henry Lingen, were making some troublesome raids, and that there was some friction between Birch and the Shropshire leadership. On 4 May the Committee of Both Kingdoms wrote to Birch:

> ... we are informed by Sir Robert Harley that since your forces were withdrawn from Herefordshire it has suffered much from the enemy, some men having been killed even at the gates of Hereford. We are also informed by the Committee of Salop that there being no other [Royalist] garrison left in that county, but only Ludlow, they will be able to take it in with their own forces. Under these circumstances, and for that the service where you are is of longer duration than we at first conceived, we think fit that you should return with your forces into Herefordshire and take care for its preservation, so soon as the Salop forces shall come up to undertake that work.[12]

A letter was also sent on the same date to Colonel Thomas Morgan, commanding the Gloucester Parliamentarian forces:

> At the desire of the gentlemen of Herefordshire, and upon intimation of some inconveniences which that county has suffered from the enemy, we have written to Colonel Birch

that upon the coming of the Salop forces to Ludlow he should march into Herefordshire. And whereas in our letter of the 15th ult. Some guns from Gloucester were ordered to be sent to him, we think these need not now be sent, and have therefore written to the Committee of Gloucester to forbear to send them.[13]

The secretariat to the Committee of Both Kingdoms were particularly busy with the affairs of Ludlow on 4 May, for a letter was also written to the Shropshire committee:

We have received your letters containing your request that Colonel Birch's forces might be withdrawn and the taking in of Ludlow left to your own forces. We have given order to him that upon the coming up of your forces and your undertaking that work, he should march into Herefordshire with his force. We recommend to your care the taking in of Ludlow, not doubting but that being your own desire, and your interest concurring with that of the public, you will use all diligence in the effectual persecution thereof.[14]

Birch's departure would have been bad news for Woodhouse, and the order was likely to prolong the siege. It is unclear when, and for how long, Birch actually left. He was still in the vicinity on 16 May, having apparently established his main siege camp in the vicinity of Steventon, two miles east of Ludlow. It is very possible that the Iron Age fort of Caynham Camp was used for this purpose.

Caynham Camp A pre-Roman fortification which was possibly the site of John Birch's camp during the siege of 1646.

Conditions within Ludlow throughout this period must have been far from normal. Unsurprisingly there were no Town Courts held after 28 April, although the council met on 4 May, and elected two new burgesses. There seem to have been few casualties among the garrison, suggesting that there was little fighting for most of the time.[15] The one notable action was when some of the horse in Ludlow made a break-out attempt, but were forced back into the town.

It is unclear if Samuel More was in command of the Shropshire forces blockading Ludlow. If he was, Woodhouse would almost certainly have been reluctant to negotiate with him. In fact, given their past history, this would probably have been impossible. It seems that discussions continued, however, with Colonels Birch and Humphrey Mackworth of the Shropshire forces taking the lead on the Parliamentarian side. Tentative agreement was apparently reached by the middle of May, before Birch left the siege, for the 20 May issue of the Parliamentarian newssheet *Perfect Diurnall* reported that:

> Letters come this day from Colonel Birch the Active Governor of Hereford and Colonel Mackworth the gallant Governor of Shrewsbury of the proceedings and Treaty for the surrender of Ludlow the only Garrison that was in Shropshire for the King; the particulars would be too long to put here. But what is more welcome we had further by letters an assurance that an absolute agreement was made for the surrender of Ludlow to be June the 1st. The officers to march away with horses and arms and common soldiers without arms. What was in the castle we'll tell you when we have it.[16]

On 27 May the *Moderate Intelligencer* confirmed the report:

> The castle and town of Ludlow we understand was delivered to Colonel Birch, who was at that siege with the Shropshire men, they had provisions of all kinds for some months, but expecting fair terms and performances out of knowledge of the said Colonel and others they yielded sooner than otherwise they needed.[17]

It seems that pending the agreed surrender date, Woodhouse and his troops may have withdrawn to the castle, and some of the Shropshire Parliamentarian forces entered the town. This could have been after Birch's departure, and possibly was in breach of the agreed conditions. Woodhouse reacted angrily:

> ... understanding that Colonel Birch was gone, before the surrender of that place according to Articles, refused to perform the same to any other, and had beat some Salopians out of the town and killed seven, whereupon Colonel Birch was sent for, being come, they resigned unto him without further dispute.[18]

As this report appeared in the *Moderate Intelligencer* of 2 June, it seems that the actual surrender at Ludlow was brought forward, probably to 30 or 31 May. The garrison will have marched to Worcester, leaving behind a large quantity of arms and munitions, including 37 cannon and the same number of barrels of powder.

The Shropshire troops killed in the final skirmish were possibly the heaviest casualties suffered in the siege, whilst the following four burials recorded in the register of St Laurence's may refer to Royalist losses: Richard Elliot, Colonel (26 April); William Holliwell, soldier (30 April); William Davies, soldier (4 May) and Ralph Bevis, soldier (1 May).[19]

For the townspeople of Ludlow, the Civil War was over. It remained to be seen how they would fare in the peace.

9   AFTERMATH

On 6 June 1646, signalling the assumption of Parliamentarian control, Colonel Samuel More, promoted from Major following his release in 1644 and made Governor of Montgomery, was appointed Governor of Ludlow.

Looking around them, the townsmen began to assess the costs of the war. Materially, Ludlow had not suffered such great damage as had other towns like Chester and, nearer to home, Bridgnorth, which had undergone prolonged and destructive sieges. Within the circuit of the town walls, there had, to be sure, been some damage. A couple of houses had been demolished in Castle Street, near the entrance to the castle, and several buildings had been burnt or demolished just within Galdeford Gate. But otherwise the inner town was largely intact.

It was otherwise in the suburbs. The main areas of destruction were in Lower Broad Street, Upper and Nether Galdeford and Upper Corve Street. For many years the records of the corporation would be dotted with references to houses destroyed in 'the late unhappy troubles', with a series of new leases issued between 1646 and 1662 for sites of corporation property. It was usual for new leaseholders to be required to 'build fair and tile' within a specified period. In 1652 Edward Turford, a glover, was expected to 'make a sufficient dwelling house and tile within five years' at 14 Corve Street.

The surviving records sometimes indicate the reasons for the destruction of a property. For example, in 1647 the 'tenement over Corve Gate ruined in these unnatural wars', and the house on the north side of Castle Street next to the town ditch 'pulled down', whilst the house of Edward Fox, on the west side of Broad Street 'below the Gate', was 'lately demolished in these unhappy wars'. One of the most notable losses was the large house built in the 16th century by the Townsend family from the ruins of St Austin's Friary, in 1654 described as 'lately burnt down'. Edward Cooke, a tailor, and possibly a Parliamentarian sympathizer as he had fled to London, had three houses 'burnt to the ground'.

The eastern side of Upper Corve Street, below the gate, seems to have been destroyed virtually in its entirety. The tax assessment for 1650 has no entries for this section of the street. Rebuilding here seems to have been slow and patchy, and apparently did not begin until about 1653. Sometimes rebuilding took decades or even centuries. On the western side of Upper Corve Street by 1672 there were still only eight houses compared with seventeen in 1641. In other cases, vacant plots were not rebuilt upon for many years, for example 51-58 Lower Broad Street, which had been the pre-war home and workplace of clothiers, and in Lower Galdeford the site of the pre-war house of Richard Browne (now the 'Queen's Head') was in 1672 'a barn and garden'. Some plots were still vacant into the 20th century.[1]

In 1647 orders were given for the demolition of the earth defences constructed during the war, signifying a gradual return to more peaceful conditions.

Parliament in Westminster remained the fairly distant influence on Ludlow life that it had been prior to the war. In a sense, with the abolition of the Council in the Marches, central government involvement with the town's day to day affairs was less. Of more immediate impact was the Shropshire County Committee, whose composition and political complexion changed according to the political and constitutional developments in the wider country. By 1648-9 with the execution of King Charles and the establishment of first the Republic and then the Commonwealth, the County Committee in turn became much more republican in membership.

Although control of municipal affairs theoretically remained with the corporation, it is evident that ultimate authority lay with the County Committee. In August 1649 it was agreed that 'the tithes of this parish and the corn growing upon the glebe have to be disposed of according to the Committee of Salop'.[2] Whilst councillors may well have grumbled, there was little in practice they could do other than go along with the new order.

The Ludlow corporation had a long tradition of bending with the political and religious breeze. It was inevitable that, following the defeat of the Royalists, a number of their leading local supporters were called to account. They were usually required to 'compound' – to pay a fine based on the value of their property and income – and to adhere to the National Covenant, thereby agreeing to observe the religious policies of the new regime. It was natural that those 'delinquents', as they were termed, brought before the County Committee which would set their level of fine to answer charges of supporting the king during the Civil Wars and, would attempt to minimise their degree of involvement with the Royalist cause, so their claims need to be treated with caution. Not all those listed were Ludlow men. Some were, for example, 'reformado' officers who had been serving with Woodhouse at the time of the town's surrender.

They included John Young, both senior and junior, of Pimbley. In 1646 the father joined the Ludlow garrison as steward of the household of the Council in the Marches. Francis Doubleday of Ebrew Farm, Middlesex, who was in Ludlow garrison when it surrendered, was fined £60. Edward Vernon of Hanbury claimed that he was imprisoned in May 1645 in Ludlow Castle by Prince Rupert and had to pay £500 for his release. Despite his plea, he was still fined £400. Sir Thomas Milward of Eaton Derbyshire, a former colonel in the Northern Horse under Sir Marmaduke Langdale, was in Ludlow when it surrendered and was fined £360, half the value of his estate. Ralph Godwin, MP for Ludlow prior to being expelled by Parliament as a Royalist on the outbreak of the war, compounded for delinquency on 7 September 1646, having been in Ludlow whilst it was garrisoned for the king. He was fined £412 10s, but the County Committee did return him his estate and cancel their lease of it.

Others listed as compounding and paying fines were Samuel Reignolds, an innkeeper who had become a Royalist officer; John Beresford, who had signed a protestation against Parliament not to have contact with the rebels; Richard Phillips, who had enlisted in Woodhouse's regiment, and John Cibbury who took up arms for the defence of Ludlow. Edward Powis (tanner), Edward and Thomas Jones (signet under clerk, Council in the Marches), Richard Wilkes (glover) and Walter Stead (mercer) were listed as captains of foot in the Royalist forces, while Samuel Weaver (haberdasher), William Langton (innkeeper), Howard Reignolds and Robert (or Roger) Kisby were listed as ensigns. John Williams was probably a major in Woodhouse's regiment, and Adam Acton (innkeeper) a lieutenant. The late Thomas Fisher, who died in 1645, had raised a company in Ludlow for the king and obtained ordnance from Bringewood Forge with which to defend Ludlow. William Colbach (shoemaker) and Charles Hawkins were noted as having been in arms at Stokesay Castle and also as having proclaimed the Earl of Essex a traitor; Thomas and Roger Powis (both tanners) as having fought against Parliament at Brampton Bryan; and Thomas son of Richard Hall (signet under clerk) as having ridden in arms.

William Bowdler (signet under clerk) of Ludlow was reported as training in arms for the king in 1646, but petitioned that he had always adhered to Parliament. On 1 October 1646, Colonel Randolph Egerton compounded for delinquency as 'being in arms', but claimed he helped secure the speedy surrender of Ludlow Castle. He was fined £411, a sixth of the value of his estate. Egerton, a Staffordshire man, had been Major-General of Horse in Charles Gerard's Royalist army in south Wales. This had largely disintegrated by early 1646, and Egerton and some remnant had evidently joined the Ludlow garrison. Thomas Jones of Ludlow, yet another signet under clerk, was reported as serving as a captain for the king and was also fined a sixth at £20.

The names of Thomas Crump senior and junior of Ludlow don't appear till 7 May 1651. The son compounded for adhering to the king at a sixth, or 20s, on 28 May. The father asked for a discharge, saying he adhered to Parliament but had lived in Ludlow when it was garrisoned for the king. Other evidence suggested that in 1646 he was a trainer in arms for the king, and that his son was an officer. Thomas Crump senior seems to have avoided a fine. Other cases of delinquency noted in 1651 included John Butts who was fined at one sixth, £33 6s 8d, two more signet under clerks Richard Gough and Cuthbert Hely, and Avery Price, a yeoman.[3]

It is significant to note that so many of these listed as delinquents had been officials of the Council in the Marches. It may suggest that financial and employment considerations weighed more heavily on their minds than political or religious allegiances.

It seems fairly clear that the majority of the corporation members had no very strong political allegiances. As a result, unlike for example in more strongly Royalist Chester, there was no wholesale purge of council members. Indeed, six of the eight bailiffs who had held office during the war remained council members, the other two having died. Two of the six, Richard Davies and Edward Turford, who had been captured by the Parliamentarians in 1645, served as bailiffs again. Although there were six new members of the corporation in 1646, five of these replaced members who had recently died. Such expulsions as there were seem to have been for non-political reasons, such as Roger Harries, who was removed in 1647 for being 'a man of very idle and vile behaviour ... chiefly towards his own wife', and Richard Dewes, expelled for 'his evil carriage towards this Corporation'.[4] Of the twenty-one bailiffs who served during the period of the Commonwealth and Protectorate, fourteen had held office before or during the Civil War.

Clearly, those individuals who had displayed clear Parliamentarian sympathies during the war stood a better chance of preferment. William Botterell had been a captain in the forces of Parliament, and afterwards would be a governor of Ludlow Castle, three times bailiff and an MP for Shropshire in the Parliament of 1653. John Aston, a mercer of clearly Puritan persuasion, was High Bailiff in 1650 and 1651, and MP for Ludlow in the Parliaments of 1654-55 and 1656-58.[5]

Although there was no large-scale settling of scores by Parliamentarian supporters, some undoubtedly took advantage of their change in fortune. In 1656, Cuthbert Hely, who had been a fairly minor official of the Council in the Marches, complained that his property in the Bull Ring had been vandalised by a group headed by John Aston, who had torn up tulips and other flowers from the garden, and replaced them with onions, before barricading the door of the 'house of office' (latrine) and frightening away his tenant.[6]

Aston was also one of those who made use of his new prominence for his own advantage. He took over what was described as 'a fair house' in Broad Street, which had previously accommodated officials of the Council in the Marches. Similarly, Thomas More, brother of Samuel, lived during the 1650s in The Feathers, whilst Sir Robert Harley, though now a moderate and out of favour with an increasingly republican regime, nevertheless took possession of Charles Fox's residence in Quality Square. None of these acts, however, seem to have involved the actual eviction of householders.[7]

The corporation displayed its willingness to bend with the wind from the outset. In August 1646 they elected without protest Thomas Mackworth and Thomas More, respectively son of Colonel Humphrey Mackworth and brother of Samuel More, as MPs for Ludlow. In November, Major William Braine – a fairly radical republican who had served in the Shropshire forces, a member of the County Committee, and in 1649 a witness at the trial of King Charles – was appointed town clerk, effectively in the role of overseer for the new regime. He held the post until his death in 1657.

Ironically, Ludlow found itself faced by higher levels of taxation than in the days of Ship Money, and administered with a good deal more efficiency by the County Committee. In April 1648, when the country was faced with the twin outbreaks of Royalist uprisings and invasion by a Scottish army now allied with the king, financial demands by the Parliamentarian authorities increased drastically. Ludlow's town clerk and John Aston were sent to the County Committee at Shrewsbury 'to endeavour to ease the town of their great assessment'. It is unlikely that they were successful, and throughout the following decade the financial costs of maintaining a large standing army fell as heavily on Ludlow as on the rest of the country. Whilst assessments were not normally as heavy as those of Ship Money, they were required much more regularly.*

The economic fortunes of the town must have been adversely affected by the abolition of the Council in the Marches, although there is no evidence of any marked increase in poverty. For example, the pre-war carrying trade – the transport of goods by wagon – seems to have resumed quite quickly after the cessation of hostilities.[9]

There were other changes reflecting the wishes of the new regime. New corporation regalia was ordered in May 1652 bearing the arms of the Commonwealth. In St Laurence's the royal coat of arms was covered with whitewash, though, perhaps significantly, not actually destroyed. The pews which were once the preserve of leading dignitaries of the Council in the Marches were now occupied by the castle governor and leading aldermen. The pipes were removed from the organ. The church bells now rang not for royal visits but for occasions such as that of 2 January 1653, when the churchwardens paid 2s 6d 'for ringing for joy when Ld. Cromwell was made Ld. Protector'. It hard to believe that the event was greeted by much real 'joy' in Ludlow.[10]

The rectors of Ludlow appointed during the Interregnum seem to have had distinct 'vicar of Bray' tendencies; at least two of them subscribed to the Anglican Book of Common Prayer reinstated in 1662. The town preachers, appointed by the corporation, were Puritans, as was William Whittall, Reader and 'Chief schoolmaster' at the Grammar School. This is not surprising; these were posts which the new regime was always anxious to fill with its supporters.[11] Throughout the period of the Interregnum County Commissions (that for Shropshire including John Aston amongst its members) were tasked with 'ejecting Scandalous Ignorant and Insufficient Ministers and Schoolmasters', and it may have been partly because of perceived unsuitability of some of the incumbents that no less than seven 'Chief Scholemasters' were appointed over a period of 11 years.

The new republican regime always ultimately relied upon military support to keep it in power. Consequently garrisons were maintained in a number of locations. Many castles were 'slighted', or partially demolished, after the war, but Ludlow Castle remained unscathed and continued to be garrisoned. Initially the garrison was provided by the Shropshire forces, although later on soldiers from the regular army replaced them. In times of crisis there were several hundred men in the Ludlow garrison.

The main task of the garrison was to guard against Royalist plots and insurrections. The most serious of these came in 1648, with the series of uprisings and the Scottish invasion known collectively as the Second Civil War. The year saw Royalist activity in Wales and the Marches, with attempts to seize Shrewsbury by conspirators led by Lord Byron. During the summer a plot was discovered 'to surprise Ludlow Castle', disclosed by Anthony Cooper, 'a soldier of the garrison who is fled from thence'.[12]

There is no evidence of involvement by the townspeople in these or any other plots, though the attitudes of some of the neighbouring gentry were more suspect. In 1651, during the future Charles II's campaign of 1651 which culminated in Cromwell's victory at Worcester, Sir Gilbert Cornewall of Burford allegedly supplied horses and men to the invaders. Following the battle, about 1,000 mainly Scottish prisoners were detained in Ludlow and other garrisons in the Marches, prior to being sent to Bristol for transportation to New England and the West Indies as indentured servants, effectively as slaves.[13] It is unlikely that their fate elicited any sympathy from the townsfolk.

In 1654 that irreconcilable Royalist, Somerset Fox of Caynham, was involved in a plot to assassinate Oliver Cromwell. The conspirators were arrested before they could put their plan into operation. Unlike some of his fellow conspirators, Fox confessed to his part in the plot, and in consequence his life was spared, although he was sentenced to be transported to Barbados. It seems probable though that the enforced exile never happened, as he was still in England in 1656.[14]

The continued Royalist unrest led to the introduction of a form of military government, with the country divided into districts under Major-Generals. The Major-General for Shropshire, Herefordshire, Worcestershire and north Wales, James Berry, had risen through the ranks of the New Model Army. In November 1655 he described Ludlow as 'that unruly town', though it is unclear whether he was referring to general disorder or political disaffection. But in the country as a whole, the rule of the Major-Generals did much to destroy support for the republican regime, and it is likely that the townspeople of Ludlow shared this feeling.[15]

Unrest continued in the Marches throughout the 1650s; the garrison was reduced in numbers for a time, but in 1659, following Oliver Cromwell's death in 1658, new Royalist conspiracies culminated in a major uprising in Cheshire under Sir George Booth against the insecure regime of Oliver's son, Richard. An additional company of foot, under Captain Edward Botterel, was ordered to be raised at a cost of £100 for the defence of Ludlow Castle, whilst the regular army crushed the revolt in Cheshire with relative ease.[16]

With an average of about 350 soldiers billeted in the town and castle, there was little that the townspeople could have done to voice their protests. Like the rest of the country, they could only hope for better times.

The death of the Lord Protector, Oliver Cromwell, in September 1658, and the uneasy succession of his son, Richard, had seen the first signs of a loosening of the republican regime. Growing discontent saw the intervention by the section of the army led by General George Monck in support of a 'freely elected Parliament', which it was generally accepted would lead to a restoration of Charles II and to a considerable extent the return of the constitutional position prior to 1641.

In the election for that Parliament in 1659, Ludlow chose Jo Charlton, who came from a strongly Royalist London family, and Samuel Baldwyn, son of the pro-Royalist Ludlow MP in the Long Parliament.

Charles II was duly restored in May 1660, and for Ludlow, May 1661 seemed to bring the final return to the retrospectively rosy times of the past, when the Council in the Marches was restored. It never regained its former prominence, however, and was finally abolished with the overthrow of the last Stuart king, James II, in the Glorious Revolution of 1688.[17]

Some of those involved in Ludlow's experience of the Civil War did not live to see the Restoration of Charles II. After his surrender in 1646, Sir Michael Woodhouse, the last Royalist governor, largely disappears from recorded history. He evidently returned to the Continent, perhaps to the Low Countries, as he is mentioned as visiting Queen Henrietta Maria at the Hague in 1647. But Woodhouse seems to have played no active part in Royalist conspiracies. According to one unconfirmed report, he died in 1651. In any case, he apparently never returned to England, and may well have met his end fighting as a professional soldier.[18]

Richard Herbert, Woodhouse's predecessor, made his peace with the new regime. He provided men and horses to oppose the Scottish invasion of 1651, and died in 1655.[19]

Somewhat surprisingly, the Florentine mercenary, John Devalier, prospered after the Restoration. By 1664 he had been knighted and was serving in Ireland. In 1670, still a professional soldier, he was a captain in the Blue Regiment of Foot.[20]

Sir Robert Harley of Brampton Bryan lost favour with the Parliamentarians because he favoured reconciliation with the king. He and his eldest son were imprisoned until after Charles' execution, and he was excluded from Parliament in 1653. Sir Robert died in 1656.[21]

Samuel More, after being a zealous and active member of the Shropshire County Committee, was accused of involvement in an attempt to depose Cromwell, and excluded as an MP until 1658. He survived the Restoration unscathed, and died in 1662.[22]

Samuel Baldwyn and Jo Charlton, Ludlow's MPs at the time of the Restoration, as proven supporters of the new regime had long and distinguished legal careers. Somerset Fox, that other dedicated local Royalist, would in his turn become MP for Ludlow.[23]

Finally, John Birch, the pragmatic conqueror of Royalist Ludlow, managed to gain for himself a rather uneasy place amongst the Herefordshire gentry. He followed a highly ambivalent political course during the Interregnum, whilst losing no opportunity to increase his own prosperity. He was with Charles II at Worcester in 1651, but cannily left before the battle began. During the Commonwealth and Protectorate he claimed to have been imprisoned no less than 21 times, but avoided any serious penalty, other than periodic exclusions as an MP. The new regime needed his support locally, for as Major-General James Berry admitted: 'the man is popular in these parts, and he loves to be so. He is taken for a great wit, and guilty of some honesty ... but he professeth desire of peace and settlement'. Birch continued his ambivalent political career for many years after the Restoration, died 'an ancient man' in 1691, and was buried in Weobley church in a somewhat grandiose tomb which encroached on the altar space.[24]

Regiments of the Ludlow Royalist Garrison[1]

The list of officers given at the end of each regiment are those who either served with the regiments during their time in Ludlow, or may be reasonably assumed to have done so.

Sir William Croft's Foot

Raised by Sir William Croft, of Croft Castle, this was principally a Herefordshire regiment. It saw action at Hereford in 1643, Brampton Bryan in 1644 and Wistanstow in 1645, where Croft was killed. It evidently included at least one company from the Ludlow area.

Captain Francis Walker (an 'ironmaster' of Clungunford, Shropshire, Walker operated an iron forge at Boulden, north-east of Ludlow, in 1643 casting ordnance and shot for the Royalist Oxford army and various garrisons)

Lieutenant Benjamin Buckley (from Shropshire, Walker's company)

John Devalier's Horse

John (more properly Giovanni) Devalier, was a Florentine professional soldier who had been a captain in Sir William Vaughan's regiment of horse on its return from Ireland in 1644. He was probably commissioned as a colonel by Prince Rupert in the summer of the same year, and became governor of Lea Hall near Bishop's Castle and later of Caus Castle. On the latter's surrender in the summer of 1645, Devalier and his men became part of the Ludlow garrison, and seem to have been quartered in the castle. In January 1646 the regiment, which never approached full strength, was reported to be attempting to recruit in Shropshire, probably with limited success. Devalier may have been at the Battle of Stow in the Wold in March 1646, although he seems to have escaped capture there.

Captain Edward Bishop (of Shropshire)

Cornet Edward Boynton (of Shropshire)

Randolph Egerton's Horse

Of Betley, Staffordshire, Egerton operated in Capel's army, and later became Major General of horse to Charles Gerard in south Wales. The unit was involved in the Royalist defeats at Rowton Heath (September 1645) and Denbigh Green (November 1645) and remnants seem to have then been in Ludlow, where Egerton was at the time of the surrender.

Richard Herbert's Foot

Raised in Shropshire and along the Welsh border (especially around Montgomery) in 1642. Originally it formed the Bridgnorth garrison. In 1643 it formed part of with Capel's army, then the Oxford army, where the regiment saw action at Bristol, Gloucester and the First Battle of Newbury. It was then part of the Ludlow garrison when Herbert was governor. The unit was at the sieges of Hopton and Brampton Bryan Castles, before accompanying Herbert to Aberystwyth in the late spring of 1644.

    Lieutenant Colonel Edward Herbert (brother to Richard Herbert)
    Major Edward Williams (commanded the regiment at Bristol, July 1643)
    Major Somerset
    Captain David Floyd
    Captain Peter Newton
    Captain Edward Price (of Shropshire)
    Lieutenant Edmund Cardiffe
    Ensign John Jervis
    Quartermaster Thomas Evans (of Shropshire)

Prince Rupert's Regiment of Foot

Not part of the Ludlow garrison as such, but with detachments often present in the town in 1644-45, this was one of the most interesting units of the Royalist army. Raised in 1642 in Somerset, under Sir Thomas Lunsford, the regiment was taken over by Prince Rupert after Lunsford's capture at Edgehill on 23 October of the same year.

    Under the operational command of Lieutenant-Colonel John Russell, the regiment saw a great deal of action during the war, fighting at the capture of Bristol and the First Battle of Newbury in 1643. It joined Rupert in the Welsh Marches early in 1644, and its veteran soldiers fulfilled a kind of 'fire brigade' role in the military operations that spring. Detachments reinforced the Royalist forces at the capture of Hopton and Brampton Bryan Castles, and it was probably mainly at this time that some were quartered in Ludlow, their failure to pay for supplies meeting with disapproval from the townspeople.

    The rank and file of the regiment were normally uniformed in blue coats, breeches and Montero caps.

    Rupert's Regiment suffered high casualties on a number of occasions, and was eventually destroyed in a spirited 'last stand' at the battle of Naseby (14 June 1645). Consequently its personnel changed considerably during the course of the war.

    Lieutenant-Colonel John Russell
    Major Dominic Mitchell
    Captain Valentine Pyne
    Captain Walwyn (of Herefordshire)
    Lieutenant Richard Walwyn (of Hereford) Walwyn's Company

Rupert also recruited a Lifeguard of Foot whilst on the Welsh Border. These red-coated troops included both European mercenaries and a strong Irish element. During Rupert's time in the Welsh Marches they were mainly stationed in the Shrewsbury garrison, but detachments may have accompanied Rupert to Ludlow.

Sir Michael Woodhouse's Regiment of Foot

The mainstay of the Ludlow garrison from the spring of 1644 to the end of the war in 1646, this regiment was raised in early 1643 in north Wales, particularly in the Denbigh area. In an effort to boost recruiting, it was originally styled 'The Prince of Wales' Regiment of Foot', although this designation seems in practice rarely to have been used. Secondary sources state that Woodhouse's was a bluecoat regiment, which is quite likely, although no contemporary confirmation has yet come to light.

The regiment saw action under Capel's command at Nantwich and Wem in the spring and early summer of 1643, without any great distinction, and was at that time mainly based at Shrewsbury.

In August it was sent to reinforce the king's Oxford army in the campaign which culminated in the First Battle of Newbury (20 September). The unit was in the thick of the fighting and suffered heavy losses. Returning to Shropshire, Woodhouse and his men were, in the spring of 1644, tasked with the capture of Hopton Castle, and took part in the killing of its surrendered garrison. From there they were despatched to assist with the capture of Brampton Bryan.

Following Sir Michael Woodhouse's appointment in April 1644 as Governor of Ludlow, his regiment formed the principal contingent of the garrison for the remainder of the war. Detachments formed part of Royalist forces in a number of actions in north Wales and the Marches, notably the Montgomery campaign (September 1644), the action at Wistanstow (June 1645) and the Battle of Denbigh Green (1 November 1645).

Following the surrender of Ludlow in April 1646, the remnants of the regiment, by now very much understrength, presumably accompanied Woodhouse to Worcester, and were disbanded following the town's surrender in June.

Lieutenant Colonel Richard Thurland (died Ludlow February 1644)

Major Edward Broughton (of Marchwiel, Denbigh). Later colonel of Trained Band-based regiment at Bridgnorth. Taken prisoner at the Battle of Stow on the Wold (21 March 1646)

Major Henry Vaughan (killed at Hopton Castle)

Major John Williams (later Lieutenant-Colonel) (of the Park, Brecon). Taken prisoner at Montgomery (18 September 1644)

Captain Oliver Broughton (of Flint)

Captain Gerard Dannet (from Herefordshire). Governor of Stokesay, June 1645

Captain Deane. Commanded detachment at Denbigh Green, 1 November 1645

Captain Ellis Phillips (of Shropshire)

Captain Richard Phillips (of Shropshire)

Captain Thomas Vaughan (killed at Hopton Castle)

Captain Lieutenant Peter Wadhall (of Northumberland)

Lieutenant Aldersley (of Ludlow). Taken prisoner at Montgomery (18 September 1644)

Lieutenant Thomas Breakes (of London and Westminster)

Robert Vaughan (of Denbigh)

Ensign Dannet Bishop (of Shropshire, Captain Dannet's Company)

Ensign Phillips

Ensign Andrew Williams (of London and Westminster, Major Williams' Company)

Quartermaster Samuel Pritchard (of Shropshire)

BIBLIOGRAPHY

Acton, Francis, Stackhouse, *The Garrisons of Shropshire During the Civil War*, Shrewsbury, 1867.

Auden, Alfred M., 'Clun and its Neighbourhood in the First Civil War', in *Transactions of the Shropshire Archaeological and Historical Society,* 3rd series, vol. 8.

Barratt, John, *Cavaliers: The Royalist Army at War, 1642-46,* Stroud, 2001
The First Battle of Newbury, 1643, Stroud, 2005
Journal of Prince Rupert's Marches, Birkenhead, 1995

Bodleian Library, *Firth MS*

Bracher, Terry, and Emmett, Roger, *Shropshire in the Civil War*, Shrewsbury, 2000.

British Library *Additional MSS* (Rupert Correspondence)

Dore, R.N. (ed), *Letterbooks of Sir William Brereton,* Record Society of Lancashire and Cheshire, 1984-1990

Eales, Jacqueline, *Puritans and Roundheads: The Harleys of Brampton Bryan and the outbreak of the English Civil War,* London, 1990.

Faraday, Michael, *Ludlow 1085-1660: a Social, Economic and Political History*, Chichester, 1991.

Farrow, W.J., *The Great Civil War in Shropshire, 1642-49*, Shrewsbury, 1929.

Gilbert, C.D., 'Clubmen in South West Shropshire, 1644-45', in *Transactions of the Shropshire Archaeological and Historical Society,* vol.68.

Gough, Richard, *History of Myddle*, 1701.

Hamilton, W.D. (ed), *Calendar of State Papers, Domestic Series,* London, 1887.

Heath-Agnew, E., *Roundhead to Royalist* (John Birch) Chichester, 1979.

Historical Manuscripts Commission, *Fifteenth Report, Marquis of Bath MSS,* vol. I, Harley Family Papers.

Hutton, Ronald, *The Royalist War Effort, 1642-1646,* London, 2nd ed. 2003.

Jones, L. (ed), 'Churchwardens' Accounts of the town of Ludlow', in *Transactions of the Shropshire Archaeological and Historical Society,* 1894.

Lewis, Thomas T. (ed), *Letters of Lady Brilliana Harley*, London, 1879.

Lloyd, David, *Concise History of Ludlow*, Ludlow, 1999.
Papers (Ludlow Historical Research Group Collection)

Lloyd, David, Clark, Margaret, and Potter, Chris, *St Laurence's Parish Church, Ludlow: The Parish church and people, 1199-2009*, Logaston, 2010.

Lloyd, David, and Johnson, Karen, *Festival Ludlow*, Logaston, 2009.

Lloyd, David, and Klein, Peter, *Ludlow: A Historic Town in Words and Pictures*, Chichester, 1984.

Long, C.E. (ed), *Diary of the Marches of the Royal Army During the Great Civil War Kept by Richard Symonds,* Camden Society, 1859.

Newman, P.R., *Biographical Dictionary of Royalist Officers, 1642-1660*, New York, 1981.
   The Old Service, Manchester, 1995.

Phillips, J.R., *Memoirs of the Civil War in Wales and the Marches, 1642-49,* London, 1874.

Phillips, William (ed), *Sir Francis Ottley's Papers*, Shropshire Archaeological and Natural History Society, 2nd and 3rd series, 1894-6, 1898, 1905

Reid, Stuart, *Officers and Regiments of the Royalist Army,* 4 vols, Southend-on-Sea, n.d.

Roy, Ian (ed), *Royalist Ordnance Papers Part II,* Oxfordshire Record Society, 1975

Ross, David, *Royalist But… Herefordshire in the English Civil War, 1642-51,* Logaston, 2012.

Shoesmith, Ron and Johnson, Andy, (eds), *Ludlow Castle: its History and Buildings*, Logaston, 2006

Shropshire County Archives, *Ludlow Corporation Records*

Train, C.J., *The Walls and Gates of Ludlow*, Ludlow, 1999

Warburton, Eliot (ed), *Memoirs of Prince Rupert and the Cavaliers,* 3 vols, London, 1849.

Webb, John, and Webb, T.W., *Memorials of the Civil War between King Charles I and the Parliament of England, as it Affected Herefordshire and the Adjacent Counties*, 2 vols, London, 1879.

Notes & References

Abbreviations used

C.S.P.D.	Calendar of State Papers Domestic
B.L.	British Library
Bod. Lib.	Bodleian Library
David Lloyd Papers	Material in the collection of Ludlow Historical Research Group.
N.L.W.	National Library of Wales
P.R.O.	Public Record Office (now National Archives)
S.R.O.	Shropshire Record Office (now Shropshire Archives)
T.S.A.S.	Transactions of the Shropshire Archaeological Society

Chapter 1

1. William Camden, *Britannia*, 1659 ed. p.386.
2. Michael Faraday, *Ludlow, 1085-1660*, Chichester, 1991, pp.1-2 provides an excellent summary of the available evidence.
3. C.J. Train, *The Walls and Gates of Ludlow*, Ludlow, 1999, *passim.*
4. Faraday, *op. cit,* especially Chapters 6 and 8.
5. *Ibid*, Chapter 5, and Penry Williams, *The Council of the Marches under Elizabeth I*, Cardiff 1958.
6. David Lloyd and Karen Johnson, *Festival Ludlow*, Logaston, 2009, p.24.
7. Faraday, *op cit*; David Lloyd, *Concise History of Ludlow*, Ludlow 2005, p.66.
8. *Ibid.*
9. P.R.O. SP46/164, ff. 50-84; Faraday, *op.cit.* p.101.
10. M.D.G. Wanklyn, *Landed Society and Allegiance of Cheshire and Shropshire in the First Civil War* (unpublished University of Manchester PhD Thesis) 1976, p.19.
11. Richard Baxter, *Reliquiae Baxterianae*, London, 1696, pp.85-6.
12. David Lloyd and Peter Klein, *Ludlow, A Historic Town in Words and Pictures,* Chichester, 1984, p.48.
13. Faraday, *op.cit.*, pp.157-70.
14. *Ibid,* pp.103-36.
15. *Ibid.*
16. *Ibid,* p.132.
17. Lloyd, *Concise History*, pp.95-98; Thomas Churchyard, *The Worthiness of Wales*, 1587, reprinted in R.H. Clive (ed) *Documents connected with the History of Ludlow and the Lord Marchers*, Shrewsbury, 1841, pp.58-88.
18. Lloyd, *Concise History,* p. 93; Faraday, *op. cit.* pp.155-6.
19. Calculation by Faraday, *op. cit.*, p.165.
20. Lloyd, *Concise History*, pp.87-94.
21. Faraday, *op.cit.*, p.37.
22. Lloyd, *Concise History, op. cit;* Faraday, *op.cit.*, pp.37-42.
23. David Powell, *The Love of Wales to their Sovereign Prince*, London, 1616, reprinted Clive, *op.cit.*, pp.58-80.

Chapter 2

1. A good introduction to this complex topic is Peter Gaunt, *The English Civil Wars, 1642-51*, Oxford, 2003
2. See Blair Worden, *The English Civil Wars 1640-1660*, London, 2010.
3. David Lloyd, Margaret Clark and Chris Potter, *St Laurence's Church Ludlow, the Parish, Church and People, 1199-2009*, Logaston, 2010, p.98.
4. *Ibid*, pp.98-106.
5. Faraday, *op.cit.*, p.45; P. Williams, *Government and Politics in Ludlow, 1590-1642*, in *T.S.A.S.* vol. 56.
6. Williams, *op.cit; C.S.P.D.*1637-8, pp.403, 450; 1638-9, p.55.
7. Faraday, *op.cit.*, p.171.
8. *C.S.P.D.* 1640, p.173.
9. Williams, *op cit.*, p.283.
10. *Ibid.*

Chapter 3

1. Mark Charles Fissell, *The Bishops' Wars: Charles I's Campaigns Against Scotland 1638-40,* Cambridge, 1994, p.195.
2. Robert Ward, *Animadversions of War*, London, 1635, p.30.
3. Richard Gough, *History of Myddle*, London, 1981 (ed) p.5.
4. *Ibid.*
5. *Ibid.*
6. Historical Manuscripts Commission, *15ᵗʰ Report*, App.II., p.104.
7. Clive Holmes, *The Eastern Association in the English Civil War*, London, 1974, p.166.
8. Anon., *Orders and Instruments of War*, London, 1642.
9. Charles E. Carleton, *Going to the Wars: The Experience of the British Civil Wars, 1638-51,* London, 1994, p.226.
10. Quoted *Ibid.*
11. W.C. Abbott (ed) *Writings and Speeches of Oliver Cromwell*, 4 vols, Oxford, 1939, vol I, p.204.

12. R.N. Dore (ed), *Letterbooks of Sir William Brereton*, Volume II, Record Society of Lancashire and Cheshire, vol. 128, 1990, items 770, 801.
13. F. Redlich, *The German Military Entrepreneur and his Workforce*, quoted in *English Civil War Notes and Queries*, no.44, p.23.
14. Dore, *op.cit.*, item 770.
15. Quoted in Sir John Fortescue, *History of the British Army,* 13 vols, London, 1910-13, vol. II, p.282.
16. *C.S.P.D.* 1644, p.24.

Chapter 4

1. *Letters of Lady Brilliana Harley,* Camden Society, 1853, p,172.
2. *Ibid.*
3. Ronald Hutton, *Royalist War Effort*, London, 2003, p.25.
4. *True Intelligence and Joyfull News from Ludlow*, B.L. E. 121 (12); J. Moxon, *The Forgotten Battle of Standard Oak*, in *Ludlow Heritage News,* 10, September 1988; John Barratt (ed), *Journal of Prince Rupert's Marches*, Birkenhead, 1995, p.3.
5. S.R.O. XLB 7/7/3/54
6. S.R.O. XLB/7/7/3/55
7. P.R. Newman, *Biographical Dictionary of Royalist Officers in England and Wales, 1642-1660*, New York, 1981, item 1602; Hutton, *op. cit.*, p.32.
8. Stuart Reid, *Officers and Regiments of the Royalist Army*, Southend-on-Sea, n.d., vol 4, p.192.
9. N.L.W. *Llanfair-Brynodol MS*, 48-50.
10. William Philip (ed), *Sir Francis Ottley's Papers,* Shropshire Archaeological and Natural History Society, 1894-6, 2ⁿᵈ series, p.86.
11. S.R.O. 356/2/1 11 May 1643.
12. *Calendar of Committee for Compounding*, p.1484 (transcript in *David Lloyd Papers*).
13. Train, *op.cit.*, pp.39-42.
14. *Ibid,* p.36.

15. The definitive work on Ludlow Castle is Ron Shoesmith and Andy Johnson (eds) *Ludlow Castle: its History and Buildings,* Logaston, 2006

16. Faraday, *op.cit,* p.174.

17. *Ottley Papers, op.cit,* p.330

18. *Ibid,* pp.342-3.

19. Quoted Hutton, *op.cit.,* p.62.

20. J. Webb, and T.W. Webb, *Memorials of the Civil War in Herefordshire,* 2 vols, London, 1879, vol I, p.320.

21. John Barratt, *The First Battle of Newbury,* Stroud, 2005, p.105.

22. Webb, *op.cit.,* p.289; Newman, *op.cit.,* item 943.

23. Ian Roy (ed) *Royalist Ordnance Papers,* Part II, Oxfordshire Record Society, vol. XLIX, 1995, item B.184.

24. *Ibid,* item C.16.

25. Newman, *op.cit,* item 719.

26. Eliot Warburton, *Memoirs of Prince Rupert and the Cavaliers,* 3 vols, London, 1849, vol I, p.513.

27. Transcript, *David Lloyd Papers.*

Chapter 5

1. B.L. *Add.MS.* 18981 f.128

2. Bod. Lib. *Firth MS.* C6. f.71

3. Hutton, *op.cit.,* p.132.

4. Transcribed *David Lloyd Papers.*

5. Paul Remfry, *Hopton Castle,* Newport, 1995.

6. H.M.C. *Marquis of Bath MS.,* Captain Priamus Davis's Account, pp.28-9.

7. *Ibid.,* Samuel More's Account, p.36.

8. *Ibid.*

9. *Ibid.*

10. Warburton, *op.cit,* vol.I, p.511.

11. *Bath MS, op.cit.,* p.30.

12. *Op.cit,* p.38.

13. *Ibid.*

14. *Ibid.*

15. An unnamed source quoted Webb, *op.cit.,* vol.II, p.371.

16. *Ibid.*

17. *Mercurius Aulicus,* 18 April 1644, p.1031.

18. *Bath MS, op.cit.,* p. 41.

19. Quoted P.R. Newman, *The Old Service,* Manchester, 1998, p.194.

20. *David Lloyd Papers.* Transcript of churchwardens' accounts.

21. *Ibid.,* transcript of St Laurence's Burial Registers.

22. *Bath MS,* p.31

23. *Ibid.*

24. Bod. Lib. *Firth MS.* C7.f. 41

25. *Bath MS,* p.31.

26. Quoted Webb, *op.cit.,* Vol II, p.359.

27. *Bath MS,* p.32.

28. *Ibid.*

29. Webb, vol II, p.360.

30. *Ibid.*

31. *Bath MS,* p.33

32. *Ibid.,* p.34.

33. Webb, vol. II, p.361.

34. *Bath MS.* p.36.

35. *Ibid,* p.38.

36. *Webb, vol.II, p.361.* Sir Richard Willys was a Royalist commander taken prisoner at Ellesmere in January.

37. *David Lloyd Papers.* Transcript of St Laurence's Burial Registers.

38. *Ibid.* Transcript of churchwardens' accounts.

39. *Bath MS,* p. 34.

40. *Ibid.,* pp.33-4.

41. *Ibid.,* p.34

42. *Ibid.*

43. *Ibid.*

44. *Ibid.*

45. *Ibid.,* p.35.

46. *Ibid.*

47. *Ibid.*

48. *David Lloyd Papers.* Transcription.

Chapter 6

1. Shoesmith and Johnson, *op.cit., passim*
2. Faraday, *op.cit,* pp.172-3; transcript, *David Lloyd Papers.*
3. *Calendar of Committee for Compounding, op.cit.*
4. *Ibid.*
5. *David Lloyd Papers.* Transcripts.
6. S.R.O. XLB7/7/56
7. S.R.O. XLB7/7/57
8. S.R.O XLB 7/7/4/5
9. S.R.O. XLB7/7/4/6
10. S.R.O. XLB7/7/4/7
11. There is no entirely satisfactory reconstruction of the unusually obscure Battle of Montgomery. The principal contemporary accounts are reprinted in J.R. Phillips, *Memoirs of the Civil War in Wales and the Marches*, 2 volumes, London, 1874, Vol. II, pp.201-9; St Laurence's Burial Register, transcribed *David Lloyd Papers.*
12. Warburton, *op. cit.* vol. I, p.530.
13. B.L. *Add MS*, 18981, f.299.
14. Mark Stoyle, *Soldiers and Strangers: an ethnic history of the English Civil War*, London, 2005, pp.93, 102-3, 117, 195, 220.
15. Bod.Lib. *Firth MS* C.7, f.224.
16. E. Stackpole-Acton, *The Garrisons of Shropshire During the Civil War*, Shrewsbury, 1867, pp.53-4.
17. *Ibid.*, p.54
18. http://www.dayofarchaeology.com/the-bitterley-hoard; Peter Reavill (Finds Officer, Shropshire Museums) personal communication.
19. Quoted in C.D. Gilbert, *Clubmen in South-West Shropshire, 1644-45,* T.S.A.H.S, vol.68. p.31.
20. Bod.Lib. *Firth MS.*, C.6, f.303.
21. Stoyle, *op.cit.*, p.195.
22. Bod.Lib. *Firth MS.*, C.6, f.332.
23. S.R.O. Transcribed *David Lloyd Papers.*
24. *Ibid.*
25. *Ibid.*
26. *Ibid.*
27. *Ibid.*
28. Warburton, *op.cit.* vol.III, pp.55-6.
29. *Ottley Papers, op.cit.,* p.294.
30. *Ibid.*
31. P.R.O. C.3/457/97. Transcribed *David Lloyd Papers.*
32. Alfred M. Auden, *Clun and its Neighbourhood in the First Civil War,* T.S.A.H.S., 3rd series, vol. 8, p.47.
33. *Ibid,* p.49.

Chapter 7

1. B.L. *Add. MS.* 18982, f.33.
2. *Journal of Prince Rupert's Marches, op.cit.,*p.14.
3. Hutton, *op.cit.* pp.170-1.
4. Dore(ed) *Letterbooks, op.cit.* Vol.I,, item.186
5. *Ibid.*
6. C.E. Long, (ed), *Diary of the Marches of the Royal Army in The Great Civil War*, Camden Society, 1859, p.168.
7. Quoted Stackhouse-Acton, *op.cit.,* p.77.
8. *Ibid;* John Lewis, *Battle of Wistanstow,* in *English Civil War Notes and Queries,* no.51, pp.8-10.
9. Lewis, *op.cit.*
10. St Laurences Burial Register, transcribed *David Lloyd Papers.*
11. Stackhouse-Acton, *op. cit.,* p.42.
12. Warburton, *op.cit,* vol III, p.184.
13. David Ross, *Royalist But… Herefordshire in the English Civil Wars*, Logaston, 2012, Chapter 15 *passim.*
14. Stackhouse-Acton, *op.cit.,* p.60.
15. Auden, *Clun, op.cit.,* p.39.
16. Warburton, *op.cit,* Vol. III, p.201.
17. Newman, *Royalist Officers, op.cit.,* item 1483. Vaughan's origins remain obscure, but the presence of a number of Radnor-

shire men in his Regiment may suggest a connection with the Vaughans of the Radnorshire-Herefordshire border.

18. Dore, *op.cit.,* vol. II, item 726.
19. *Ibid.*, item 770.
20. Long, *op.cit.*, p.181.
21. Dore, *op. cit.,* item 802; for the battle see *Ibid,* Appendix VIII.
22. *Ibid,* item 811.
23. Hutton, *op.cit,* p.193.
24. Dore, *op. cit.*, item 843.
25. *Ibid,* item 861; Stackhouse-Acton, *op.cit.,* pp.78-9.
26. Dore, *op cit.,* item 1089.
27. *C.S.P.D.* 1645-7, p.164.
28. *Ottley Papers, op.cit.*, p.294.
29. Newman, *Royalist Officers, op.cit.*, item 414.

Chapter 8

1. *C.S.P.D.* 1645-7, p. 397.
2. *Ibid.*
3. D.N.B, *John Birch*
4. *Perfect Occurrences*, transcribed *David Lloyd Papers.*
5. S.R.O. 356/2/1.
6 Notes and Map, *David Lloyd Papers.*
7. Faraday, *op.cit.,* p.179.
8. B.L. *T.T.E.* 336 (13)
9. *Ibid.*
10. *C.S.P.D.* 1645-7, p.412.
11. *Ibid.*
12. *Ibid.,* p.431.
13. *Ibid.,* p.432.
14. *Ibid.,* p.434.
15. Faraday, *op. cit,* p. 176.
16. *Perfect Diurnal*, no.143, transcribed *David Lloyd Papers*
17. *Moderate Intelligencer*, no.64, transcribed *David Lloyd Papers.*
18. *Ibid,* no.65, transcribed *David Lloyd Papers.*

19. St Laurence's Burial Register, transcribed *David Lloyd Papers.*

Chapter 9

1. *David Lloyd Papers;* Faraday, *op.cit.,* pp.178-80
2. Faraday, p.178.
3. *Calendar of Committee for Compounding,* Vol.II, transcribed *David Lloyd Papers.*
4. Faraday, p.177.
5. *Ibid.*
6. *Ibid.*
7. *David Lloyd Papers.*
8. *Ibid.*
9. *Ibid.*
10. Lloyd, Clark and Potter, *op.cit.*
11. Faraday, *op. cit; David Lloyd Papers.*
12. *C.S.P.D.* 1648, transcribed *David Lloyd Papers.*
13. *Ibid.*
14. *Ibid.*
15. *David Lloyd Papers.*
16. *Ibid.*
17. *Ibid.*
18. Newman, *Royalist Officers, op.cit.*
19. *Ibid.*
20. *Ibid.*
21. *D.N.B.*
22. *Ibid.*
23. *Ibid.*
24. *Ibid.*

Appendix

1. Information for these units is drawn mainly from Stuart Reid, *Officers and Regiments of the Royalist Army,* (Southend on Sea, n.d.); *A List of Officers Claiming to the Sixty Thousand Pounds &c. Granted by His Sacred Majesty for the Relief of His Truly-Loyal and Indigent Party*, London, 1663; author's files.

INDEX OF SUBJECTS

Index of People and Places

(Page numbers in italics refer to illustrations)

Also from Logaston Press

The Churches of Shropshire & their Treasures
by John Leonard

This book is an updated edition of that first published in 2004, to a new design and now includes just under 500 colour photographs. It explores 320 Shropshire churches, from those with Anglo-Saxon origins to ones built in the last few decades. The first chapters consider various aspects of their foundation, architecture, decoration, furnishings and monuments, whilst later chapters take a geographical area of the county and describe each church within that area, highlighting what is of particular interest. A starring system is used to indicate which churches the author feels offer most to a visitor.

The Drovers Roads of the Middle Marches
by Wayne Smith

This is the story of the men who until as recently as the 1930s used to walk with their sheep and cattle out of Wales along the ancient trackways to the markets and fairs of England. The journeys were carefully judged – too slow and the expenses of feeding and accommodating men and beasts would mount, too fast and the animals would lose condition. Taking the easier routes meant the expense of turnpikes and tollgates, but going the long way round cost time. Droving was a steady trade, and the drovers were often entrusted with commissions and even money to be taken to London, a practice from which the first banks developed. Tell-tale signs of droving routes can still be discerned in the landscape in the pine trees and ponds that marked the routes, and the names of farms, houses and inns. Wayne Smith describes the routes the drovers took, and includes sections in 16 circular walks, all illustrated with his own photographs.

The Herefordshire School of Romanesque Sculpture
by Malcolm Thurlby

This book, first published in 1999, has been much enlarged and extended. The new edition is almost double the length, is in a larger format, is printed in colour and includes a history of the Anarchy in Herefordshire by Bruce Coplestone-Crow.

This vibrant collection of work was carved between *circa* 1134 and 1155 by a group of sculptors who, it would seem, had received their initial training at Hereford Cathedral. This book explores their work, considering the careers of the two main sculptors, the role of the patrons, the sources of inspiration, the coming together of the work of the sculptor with that of the metalworker and the illuminator and painter, and the intended meaning behind some of the imagery. As the authors explain, the sculptors were working in the days of the Anarchy, and at times they were working on or near the front line between the opposing factions supporting Stephen or Matilda. Strange as it may seem, the patrons of the work were also warlords.